"This is one of the greatest storytellers any of us have ever come across in our lives"
Bono (musician)

"He never hides his intelligence, he's an incredible songwriter"
Sting (musician)

"He sings of real things. Real life. With 'I Don't Like Mondays' he connected with the American people like a Neil Young or a Bob Dylan. Sometimes people don't get it. But we need more of it"
Paul Rappaport (ex-Vice-president, National Radio Promotion, Columbia Records)

"He's probably the greatest person I've met at looking truth directly in the face, and that's not easy for the truth is an ugly thing"
Jools Holland (musician, broadcaster)

"Geldof comes from the Beatles school of song-writing. What happens to you that day, that moment can be a song. Can be a hit song"
Paul Gambaccini (broadcaster)

"It would truly be impossible to write a social history of late 20th Century Ireland without quoting 'Banana Republic'. It's the 'Easter 1916' (W.B. Yeats) of its day to me"
Joseph O'Connor (author, lecturer)

"I knew then, and I know now that 'I Never Loved Eva Braun' is one of the greatest pop songs ever written and that *A Tonic For The Troops* is a pop masterpiece"
Neil McCormick (music writer, Daily Telegraph music critic)

"The Boomtown Rats first album sees Geldof speak for our generation, 'Looking After No. 1' is Ireland's 'My Generation' These are songs of a dispossessed people"
Eoin Devereux (Professor of Social Sciences)

"They are phenomenally catchy songs"
Charles Shaar Murray (music writer)

"Geldof is a great songwriter. These are very sophisticated songs"
Dave Stewart (musician, producer, songwriter)

"Amazing songs. I was 17. 'Looking After No. 1' woke me up"
Alan McGee (founder, Creation Records)

"Brilliant writing. He comes from the tradition of the angry young poet, writing songs that expose people who are turning blind eyes. His songs were always more literate than the English punks... they were ... well they were more Irish!"
Roy Foster (Professor of Irish History, Oxford University)

"There are only two pop artists in our list this year, Leonard Cohen and Bob Geldof"
BBC, The Nations Favourite Poet (as reported in The Times, 1990)

"There's few of the newer generation that can be considered lyricists of worth. Amongst them might be Bryan Ferry, Bob Geldof... etc."
Robert Sandall (Sunday Times)

"Bleak, spooky and unsettling"
Evening Standard

"The problem for Geldof is that his puns, references and wordplay may simply be too intelligent for the average rock audience"
The Village Voice, New York

"Lyrically there is always a nakedness that takes the breath away"
The Daily Telegraph

Bob Geldof

tales of Boomtown glory

Faber *ff* MUSIC

Were you thinking that those were the words, those upright
   lines? those curves, angles, dots?
No, those are not the words, the substantial words are in
   the ground and sea,
They are in the air, they are in you.
A Song Of The Rolling Earth
Walt Whitman

This book is dedicated to...

The Boomtown Rats: Pete, Simon, Garry, Gerry, Johnnie
And Alan and Darren

And to The BobKatz: J.T, Vince, Jim, Niall
And Paul

And to every other musician and producer whom I have worked or played with and who has helped breathe life into these words

Contents

13 Introduction
17 Foreword

19 10:15
20 $6,000,000 Loser
21 A Full Moon Over Addis
22 A Gospel Song
23 A Hold Of Me
25 A Hole To Fill
27 *Notes: Love, Loss and Memory*
31 A Rose At Night
32 A Second Time
33 A Sex Thing
35 A Storm Breaks
36 A Summer Day – London '05
37 Against The Whole World
38 An Icicle In the Sun
41 *Notes: Another Piece of Red*
42 Another Piece Of Red
43 *Notes: Attitude Chicken*
45 Attitude Chicken
48 August Was A Heavy Month
50 Baby's Going Down
51 Back To Boomtown
54 *Notes: Banana Republic*
57 Banana Republic
58 Banker's Song, The
59 Battersea Morning
60 Beat Of The Night, The
62 Before The Day Begins
63 Big Romantic Stuff
64 Bitter End, The
65 Blind Date
66 Blow Hateful Wind
67 Blowfish
68 Blue Balloons

CONTENTS

69	*Notes: The Boomtown Rats*
72	Boomtown Rats, The
73	Born To Burn
74	Bright Lights Of Dublin, The
75	Can't Stop
77	Chains Of Pain, The
78	Charmed Lives
79	Cheerio
80	Close As You'll Ever Be
81	Cool Blue And Easy
83	Crazy
84	Crucified Me
86	*Notes: Dave*
89	Dave
91	Dazzled By You
92	Deep In The Heart Of Nowhere
93	Diamond Smiles
95	Dig A Ditch
97	*Notes: Do The Rat*
99	Do The Rat
101	*Notes: Band Aid...*
102	Do They Know It's Christmas?
103	Doesn't Matter Now
104	Doin' It Right
105	Don't Believe What You Read
106	Don't Talk To Me
107	Drag Me Down
108	*Notes: Drive On Damo*
109	Drive On Damo
110	*Notes: The Elephant's Graveyard*
112	Elephant's Graveyard, The
114	End Of The World, The
115	*Notes: Europe Looked Ugly*
117	Europe Looked Ugly
118	Fall Down
119	Fanzine Hero
121	Fields Of Spring, The
123	*Notes: For Those Who Travel Lonely...*
124	For Those Who Travel Lonely...
125	Friends For Life
126	Get A Grip...

127	Go
128	*Notes: Go Man Go!*
130	Go Man Go!
132	Good Boys In The Wrong
133	Great Song Of Indifference, The
135	Happy Club, The
136	*Notes: Hard Times*
137	Hard Times
139	Harvest Moon
141	Having My Picture Taken
142	He Watches It All
143	Her Turn Tonight
144	Here's A Postcard...
146	Here's To You
147	Hotel 75
149	House At The Top Of The World, The
151	House On Fire
152	How Do You Do?
153	How I Roll
156	Huge Birdless Silence
157	Hurt Hurts
159	I Can Make It If You Can
161	I Cry Too
163	I Don't Like Mondays
164	*Notes: Eva Braun*
168	(I Never Loved) Eva Braun
169	I Want You
171	In The Pouring Rain
173	Inside Your Head
174	It Doesn't Have To Be That Way
176	*Notes: It's 3*
177	It's 3
178	It's All The Rage
179	It's Been A Good Life
181	*Notes: Joey*
184	Joey's On The Streets Again
186	Johnny Nogood
187	Just Get On
188	Keep It Up
189	K.I.S.S.
191	Kicks

CONTENTS

192	Late Last Night
194	Let It Go
195	Life Is The Hardest Thing
196	Like Clockwork
198	Like Down On Me
200	Little Death, The
202	Living In An Island
203	*Notes: Lookin' After No. 1*
205	Lookin' After No. 1
207	*Notes: Love Like A Rocket*
209	Love Like A Rocket
211	Love Or Something
213	Lying Again
215	Mary Of The Fourth Form
216	Mary Says
217	Maybe Heaven
219	Me And Howard Hughes
221	*Notes: Ménage À Trois*
222	Ménage À Trois
223	Mind In Pocket
224	Monster Monkeys
225	Mood Mambo
230	Mudslide
233	My Birthday Suit
234	My Blues Away
235	My Hippy Angel
237	Neon Heart
238	Never Bite The Hand That Feeds
239	Never In A Million Years
240	New Routine, The
241	Nice 'N' Neat
242	Night Turns To Day
244	No Hiding Place
245	No Small Wonder
246	No Tomorrow Like Today
248	Nothing Happened Today
250	One For Me
252	One Of The Girls
254	Original Miss Jesus, The
255	Out Of Order
258	Over Again

CONTENTS

260	Pale White Girls
262	Passing Through
263	Pity The Poor Drifter
264	Please Don't Go
265	Pulled Apart By Horses
266	Put Out The Cat
268	*Notes: Rat Trap*
271	Rat Trap
273	Ratified
274	Ratlife
275	Real Different
277	Roads Of Germany
279	Rock 'n Roll YéYé
280	*Notes: Room 19*
283	Room 19 (Sha La La La Lee)
284	Say Hi To Mick
285	Scream In Vain
286	She Said NO.
287	She's A Lover
288	(She's Gonna) Do You In
289	She's Not The Best
290	She's So Modern
291	Shine On
292	Sighs And Whispers
293	Silly Pretty Thing
295	Skin On Skin
297	So Strange
299	Soft Soil, The
301	Someone's Looking At You
303	Song Of The Emergent Nationalist, The
305	Straight Up
307	Summers Evening (London '05)
308	Sweet Thing
309	Systematic 6-Pack
310	Talking In Code
311	Thinking Voyager 2 Type Things
313	This Heartless Heart
315	This Is My Room
316	This Is The World Calling
318	To Live In Love
321	Tonight

CONTENTS

323	Too Late God
325	Too Late She Cried
326	Trash Glam Baby
327	Truly, True Blue
328	Two Dogs
329	Under Their Thumb (Is Under My Thumb)
330	Up All Night
331	Vegetarians Of Love, The
333	Voodoo Child
336	Walking Back To Happiness
338	Walking Downtown
340	(Watch Out For) The Normal People
341	When I Was Young
344	When The Night Comes
346	*Notes: Wind Chill Factor (Minus Zero)*
348	Wind Chill Factor (Minus Zero)
350	Women In My Life, The
351	Words From Heaven
352	Yeah, Definitely
353	Young And Sober
355	Index of first lines

Introduction

The words come. Or they don't, but they will. You hope. And then they arrive, blessedly. A Gabriel-like visitation, whispering in the Virgin's head that something will be born that will rock the cradle of the world. Which would be nice, except the words turn out to be clunky, laboured, struggled for and wrestled with and ultimately become impossible to sing. Or just plain drivel. Then you must close your eyes, sit back into the tune and melody and chords and drift away into what this THING is and what it is suggesting to you. What's it for? Why did you start playing *this?* What's it *about?* What are you signalling? What are you trying to *tell* yourself? And standing at the mic you panic. The backing track is finished. You've tried to put off doing the overdubs for as long as possible. But the soloists need to have some clue as to what *they* can play. What the mood/feel/thought behind the half-finished thing is. The tape rolls. The track begins. The beat is counted in. The intro expires and you... Well, you open your gob and hope for the best. Unbelievably sometimes it works. In its panic, the subconscious hurls a Morse code of imagery and language and phraseology that is vomited into the foreconscious, which has no time to query or rationalise what it is saying, never mind actually meaning, before it grabs the mash-up of vowels and grunts and sounds and noises and it commands your mouth to say it. You listen back and it *feels* right, it *sounds* right, it *is* right, but it is only much later – perhaps years after – before you will understand what it *means.* Why you needed to say it. If only for yourself.

Course other times it just spills out of you. Start to finish – done. Or it hangs around unresolved, half done in a notebook or your head. Waiting frustratedly to be born. Or stillborn. Or it looks good on paper but it just doesn't work with the music. But one day, one day...

Or there's a character or an avatar of a character and you give them a life. Just for 3-and-a-half minutes. Just long enough for them to live, breathe and tell their précised story at your will. They make their point and they exit the stage. But they will be back the next night, at the next town, on the next stage, where they will parade their wild horse one more time.

Lyrics are not poems. For proof, try the 'out-loud test'. Reading a song lyric aloud, howsoever profound it may be to your personal life,

INTRODUCTION

to most everyone else it seems a bit lame. Or simply stupid. Unless you're 15. But everything's important at 15. As it should be.

For sure there are lines in rock that are as incandescent as anything written by the poetic greats. But they are just that, a few lines. The complete song, however, may ultimately leave you as moved as the greatest poem. It is not a lesser form. Leonard Cohen is an okay poet but a great lyricist. Bob Dylan's earlier songs are awful poetry but superb lyrics with poetic *sounding* imagery. Pop doesn't have to *make* sense it just has to *feel* sense. It inhabits an emotional intelligence rather than a rational or intellectual or empirical one.

Lyrics don't have to be *about* anything. A truth or an apparent truth that can be beyond actual meaning. Coherence is not required. What is required of a song lyric is an idea that fits around the music (or vice versa) rather than any metaphoric or practical reasoning. And therein lies the difference between the poet and the lyricist. It's the tune, stoopid!

Poets have the sound of the words and the rhythm of the lines and that is the 'music' of a poem. Everything the poet means to say must be contained in the entirety of his words. But in rock, pop, opera or any other music where instrumentation is present, lyrics are reductionist. There is no need necessarily for them to be over elaborate or grand. They can be, but in essence the psychology of a song, its meaning and sense are conveyed by the melody and the underlying sub-structure of rhythm, beat, choice of instrumentation, note selection, 'feel', metre, scansion, tempo, etc.

The simplest songs, the roughest, repetitive blues moans that well up from some primordial universal human experience, can bring you to tears. Why? The words are spare, often to the point of being hardly words. Often making no joined-up sense whatsoever. Often not *being* words at all. Quantum words. Words that never existed before and until you heard them.

I have said that rock 'n' roll is an articulate form of inarticulacy. When words fail, music can oftentimes express that which is otherwise inexpressible. As Noël Coward wrote in 'Private Lives': "Strange how potent cheap music is."

"AWOPBOPALOOPBOPALOPBAMBOOM" means nothing but says it all – wish I'd written that! But so does every other writer in rock... Rolling Stone magazine voted it 'the most inspired rock lyric ever'. Why? Because it's an articulated drum beat. Because it's a sexual howl. Because it's a roar of frustrated hope and exclusion. Because it's a beautiful black boy saying I'm here, I'm not invisible, I'm not going

INTRODUCTION

away, I'm in your face and I'm black, I'm beautiful, I'm gay and I'M COMING. Long before James Brown got there, Little Richard said it loud – "I'm black and I'm proud!!"

But here's the lyric thing. He didn't have to *say* it, he just screamed a brilliant made-up wordnoise and it was universal. Everyone got it. Whatever the deal was at that time in your life – then or now – you kind of went "fuckyea!!!" Forget English, this 'word' was a hit everywhere. Turned out the lingua franca of the planet was neither English, Spanish or Mandarin but Rock 'n' Roll. And I remembered that when it came time to do Live Aid.

Still, it will never be as simple again as in those earliest days. Pop grew up, moved on and found other more complex ways of expression, both musical and lyrical. And yet the hardest thing is to be simple. To strip back, strip down, shave and pare to some pure essence of sense. Then again, often you don't want to. You want to tell a story or a narrative or just work things out.

I'm so lucky I get to do this, I'm so lucky I'm able to do this. I literally mean that I don't know what I would do without the ability to make my world understandable through words and music. My novelist friend says that he uses his books to put a frame of reference around the things that have happened to him. That's me. When things happen that are incomprehensible and vast and borderless in their pain or grief or joy or loss I can – often unconsciously – work it out or through, in some song. Then my tired heart or racing mind or battered soul vomits or ekes into my head and onto a page/tape/guitar something that will perhaps allow me to begin to comprehend or understand or rationalise or contextualise my vagrant life, my pilgrim soul.

I have written countless, thousands upon thousands of words in books, articles, essays, speeches, stuff I think are poems (!!!) and there are some songs. These are the recorded ones. Or one day will be recorded ones (maybe). I literally have boxes and plastic supermarket bags stuffed with pages, very early adolescent 'songs', scraps, notes of stuff I thought was the start of something or relevant in some way that one day I could use. Sometimes I randomly pull them out to have a look and sometimes the original thrill sparks anew. Most often though they are momentary flashing glimpses of their time and I put them back. For there will be more.

The ones that follow in these pages are also rooted in their moment and time. They are necessary exigencies of their musical moment. Some read okay, others are mortifying, so I plead to imagine music with them if they are to work, for that is the context in which they

TALES OF BOOMTOWN GLORY   15

INTRODUCTION

were written. Some are good, bad, sad, funny, ribald, dirty, loving, awful, tragic, bitter, scathing, cynical, barbarous, angry, sceptical, political, declamatory, apologetic and often incomprehensible (to you!). Some are just me, and some conjure old friends: Joey, Billy, Eva, Howard, Diamond, Magenta and others unnamed, and only I know who they are.

I would like for the songs you are familiar with to make more sense once read, but I fear the concrete reality of them in naked print reduces them to the merely prosaic. They never were, for me. If you do not know the accompanying tunes, most may seem bewilderingly obtuse or pathetically inept, but maybe this will prompt you to search for the record where hopefully all will be revealed. Lyrics are de-contextualised words; orphaned words snatched from their parental melodies and music; acrimonious divorcees separated by print from their musical partners. They are to be sung not spoken. Heard not read. Felt rather than understood.

But anyway, throwing all caveats aside, here they are. These are the words that got me out. That enabled my escape. The words that gave me this life. And for all their bumps and grinds I am deeply grateful to them for that.

Bob Geldof, July 2019

Foreword

The problem of being asked to write a few notes for this book on some of the songs is that I can only ever write about the ones that are based on an empirical reality; those where I was referencing tangible things that had sparked a thought process and a song line. And because those tunes are rooted in an actual moment I can remember when and how the impulse to write occurred. I've written about a few of them for the purposes of this book but that is not to impart undue importance or weight to them. They were just the first ones that threw up a postcard of the time for me. The other unexplained ones mean just as much. To me, anyway... Those written about are usually, but not exclusively, songs for the seven The Boomtown Rats albums.

That is not true of songs that are articulated sense, which are more often from my solo tracks. Feelings either known and coherent or with inchoate and often unwanted impulses forcing their way up from the pit and demanding to be understood, or at least recognised. Those senses that cannot be articulated other than through seemingly obscure lines. Often I have no idea what the lines 'mean' or why these specific words occur, but upon writing them I know for absolute certain that they are true.

I often want them to go away to avoid provoking sadness or fear within me. But the fact is that those feelings were there. I was simply and purposely ignoring them for fear of negotiating with them and acknowledging that they spoke of things better left unacknowledged or buried or unrecognised. Like forebodings that things are not right. Like the unconscious is seeing and sensing things that are so tiny that they won't bother you until they have pieced together all the little specks of clues floating around out there like life-motes and added them up into a sad warning that, like it or not, will blurt its way out of your mouth. Like a soul detective or something forcing an involuntary admission of who and what you actually are and where things are really at. Things that the operating foreconscious is too busy to recognise in its dull but necessary quotidian tasks. Slight changes of tone or mood or behaviour. Like there are problems that need addressing. Like You or Her or They are unhappy or behaving out of character. Or so you think. That although you didn't know it or were aware of it, Love or anything had somehow taken a turn.

What?... When?... How?... Or watch out, cos here comes something... What, though?

Often and very bizarrely these songs are prescient to the point of spookiness. Only when some occurrence has passed do you realise that you wrote or foretold it many months or years before. And oh, there are so many of those. Ones I cannot speak or write of, for fear of weeping. Again. I cannot listen to those ones. They are way, way too real. Recording them was unbearable (and embarrassing naked self-revelation in front of strangers not being my strong suit). But I was lucky cos Pete Briquette from the Rats was the producer of many of these tracks and he's been my friend and collaborator for some 40 years now and he knows me intimately, as I him and our often-shared lives. So then it's okay to just get on with it.

Live, you can be objective and say, "Yea I really like that one, let's do that one tonight." But then you play it and it's all just too much. Conjured up in the specific sounds of the instruments and words you once again re-live the best-forgotten and harrowing images and sadnesses and griefs and ... you may be overwhelmed with just ... too much.

So, I cannot speak to those songs, but I don't think I need to. As you leaf through this anthology you will see them, recognise them and though, like me, you may not get what I'm on about, you will understand.

And of all of the tunes I've done, these (counter-intuitively) are among my favourites of all.

10:15

Jeanne saved my soul again last night.
She bathed me in love
She told me I was beautiful
And I made her come a lot.
She made me special perfumed tea
Went and bought patisserie.
Put on music... Bob Marley
Lay me back. And fed me.

She read a poem by Baudelaire
Sitting naked in a chair.
Her perfume filled the holy air.
And eased my tired heart.
She lit a fire later on
Put her bra and panties on.
I watched her as her beauty shone.
And filled my empty soul.
And though I did my best and tried.

Sadness claimed me and I cried.
She wiped the wetness from my eyes.
Being kind, she said she didn't mind.
She drew a bath and washed me clean.
Then kneeling took me by degrees.
She held me till I went to sleep
Then put me on the 10:15.

God you work in wondrous ways.
Bless this girl for all her days.
And when I'm old and tired and grey.
I'll think of this day.
Smiling.

BOB GELDOF

$6,000,000 Loser

Take my head and fuck with it
Put it back again
We've got the technology
Put it back again
The $6,000,000 loser
Rides again

A very old friend

Hey baby are you up for pumping
Hey baby let's go bumping
Hey baby are you up for humping
Hey baby let's go jumping
Cos I...
Oh I...

A Full Moon Over Addis

There's a full moon over Addis tonight
It's so soft
It's so clear
And so bright
Let's go stand on that hill
Staring perfectly still
At that full moon over Addis tonight

Eucalyptus trees perfume the air
Casting shadows lit by the moons glare
As wild wolves howl and kill
We'll stand perfectly still
Under a full moon over Addis tonight

Can you smell the rain they're expecting this evening
It'll damp down the earth and allow you to breathe
Let's get out the car and we'll drive to the edge of the city
And we'll climb up that hill and we'll stare at that moon through the trees

Under a full moon over Addis tonight...

BOB GELDOF

A Gospel Song

If you see her say hello
If she asks how I'm doing let her know
If she says is he O.K. say it's slow
But he's coming round
And if you sleep with her
Through the darkest night
And you wake beside her in the early light
Kiss her gently like I might
And bring her round

If she stumbles if she trips and slows
In the darkest rain or through the driving snow
Bring her straight here
I'll be on my own
But bring her round

And every dream and every shadow that you heard
Will make you want to cry
In a big bad world

If you want her let her know
If she's leaving let her go
All of this will pass but it passes slow
And you'll come around
When the wind blows through October skies
And you wake up in the cold twilight
And you stretch your hand out
And there's nothing there but the night
And the darkness is all around

When the rain falls from the blackened sky
There's a heart breaking but it feels alright
See I should have done something but I let it slide
And I'll come around

A Hold Of Me

What's the story?
What's the score?
What'd we do?
What're we guilty of?
Will they shoot you down?
Bring you to your knees?
Until you hit the ground
Kick you in the teeth?

And I was standing
On my own
Staring out
Into the twilight zone
And I dreamed the icebergs
And I dreamed the heat
And my face was melting
In the acid rain

Then I was kneeling
On a stone
And I heard you scream
Into the telephone
Then I felt the hunger
So I bit the meat
And if it wasn't you
Then it must've been me

And I don't like them anymore
The things they do
The things they stand for
Shoot you down
Bring you to your knees
And when you hit the ground
Kick you in the teeth

No they'll never,
Get a hold of my heart
No they'll never,
Get a hold of me

BOB GELDOF

And the rain was falling
All around my head
And I blinked my eyes
So I wasn't dead
And my ears was ringing
And my tongue stuck out
And I licked my lips
Until my teeth fell out

And I saw you running
And you made the line
Then it was night
But it was still too bright
And then it turned to dawn
And it soon grew dark
And the streets were empty
And it was time to start

And I'm for thinking
Between the ears
For mental process
For cogs an' gears
I'm for flesh
And I'm for mind
I'm for people
I'm for life

A Hole To Fill

Everybody's got a hole to fill
It doesn't matter if your name is Jack or Jill
Everybody's got a hole that they need filled

You wake up
Time stops
Pretty soon the penny's going to drop
There's a daytime
But there's a night sky
And you think there's something wrong
But you don't know why
Still you wake up
Dry your eyes
You feel the strength to carry on awhile
And if there's one world and there's one voice
You should hear them singing above the noise,

Everybody's got a hole to fill

I left the pub last night
And I was just in time
To see them break my windows
And slash my tyres
I'm a liberal I thought
As I felt my anger rise
I was desperately searching
For my feminine side
But my feminine side
Was on her morning coffee break
I beat the shit out of one
And it felt great
Hey Bob, he said don't get annoyed
We all find different ways
To fill up the void
And I said yeah

Everybody's got a hole to fill

A Hole To Fill
(alternate verse)

She wakes up
Still looking lost
And says what's the point of this
And I say not a lot
Still she gets up
And through her weary smile
She tries to find the strength
To carry on awhile
Two days ago
She wrote away
To a mail order guru
Her postal sage
Who promised answers
By return of mail
Explaining why
Sometimes it seems
The world has failed
He wrote back
"Everybody's got a hole to fill."

Love, Loss and Memory

"Once a year he remembers that scene/But it seems so long ago now/He tries to remember more but he can't/ You don't look back/ Memories – they're like a rose that blooms at night" ('A Rose At Night')

I like that one. I like doing it on stage. Latterly a lot of the tunes are a consequence of memory. Of course, all that is just a function of age. Because at a certain point Life has accumulated so much 'stuff' that it is taking up huge amounts of neural bandwidth. Headspace. Often I wish it didn't. I wish the ghosts of the past just stayed where they were and lay still. Not much you can do about it, though. They will have their moment and wreak regret or wonder and laughter or loss and pain or questioning. And mostly I just wish my head would leave me alone.

When the Rats broke up in '86, by definition the songs became much more personal. I was on my own. I was older. There was other stuff going on. And the nature and style of the writing changed with the concerns and subject matter. So, there were times (still are) when I had a backing track (i.e. just the band playing the music), and the words that I thought had accompanied the melody that I heard in my head just don't 'fit'. Like, they're too clunky. Too literal. They don't flow with the tune, rather they impede it and it all sounds wrong somehow. Then I'll close my eyes and let whatever it is that's nagging at the bowels of my senses with a sort of urgent necessity – like a vomit rising in your gorge – y'know, like an involuntary but necessary and welcome spasm of release – I'll let it speak. And often it will make no 'sense' but it is true. It feels right. It glides and slots effortlessly into place alongside its sister tune as smooth as DNA bases on their double helix.

'The House At The Top Of The World' is a good example. Rick and Karl from Underworld had taken the backing track from another of my tunes and reversed it, that is played the tape backwards and then added organ and stuff. It was pretty and I felt that thing, that shiver of nascent recognition I've just described. Possibly because it was running backwards it suggested reverse gear, going back, memory, and because it was so pretty maybe I thought of my pretty girl back then, pre-everything and her cosy house and odd but lovely parents. And a mad sensory jumble of old friends and events and landscape from around there, and random stuff that unconsciously knowingly automatically conjured that jigsaw memory into a kind of self-addressed postcard from the psyche.

I didn't write anything down. I closed my eyes, let the track roll and spoke my heart. And oh what a pretty thing it is. If I listen now – and I never listen to old songs, save to re-learn them (I *always* hear that they are wrong. That we blew it. That they are now *much* better than when we realised them on tape, etc.) – I am hurled back to the then of that time, and I like the actual words my brain chose in the instant of recording. I like the structure the phrases automatically took to slide into the phrases of the track, I love the cumulative impressions that are slowly constructed and the pithy joy to sum it all up. I felt a great sense of 'completion' when the tape had stopped and we listened back. It is a piece of fleeting soul-smoke captured of an instant and made forever.

'The Great Song Of Indifference' is another. It started off as a laugh. I played a little finger-picking 'Irishy' jig thing and thought, "Hello, something going on here," and kept going, the band joining in on the instant. The words arrived, initially bog-standard, prosaic but somehow 'telling' to the subconscious and wherever I was at personally at that moment, though I may not have known it. The song unwound itself into some other character and finally into what is really a 'protest' song. I guess the jaunty, devil-may-care nature of the music suggested a cynic who just didn't give a fuck. What you hear on the track is by and large precisely what happened at the very instant of recording. Made up on the spot and now years later that tune has been recorded in 18 separate languages. Mad. The recording artists all send me their re-written words for approval. I always say yes. Why not? If they can use it – great! But interestingly each national 'take' on the song is usually a snapshot of whatever concerns the people of that country may have at that moment. But me? I just made it up.

I trust myself a lot now to use the same method. Close your eyes. Relax into the song. What's it telling you? Speak it. Sing it. Most often it doesn't work and I'll revert to what I've written, but sometimes it's spot on. Especially when there are no words to describe what it is I am feeling. Or if there *are* words then they seem inadequate. Or I am inadequate in finding the words I need. But too often Love and its awful cost are just too much for me. I am pulled up sharp as to my inadequacies. You reach for the heightened language of poetry and genius (for me, Keats, Yeats, Whitman, Dickinson, Larkin) to try to express it. And often that too fails, so profound is your despair.

Loss has been my sidekick these later years. The pain and grief that accompanies him are universe wide and black hole depthless. It knows no boundary. It has no known edge. It travels alongside you, packed into whatever available space there is left inside your pain-sodden, grief-laden mind. It unpacks its suitcase of tears any time but most often at the most unexpected and unwanted moments. And then, once again, you're sliding down the ladder to that damp, dark, bottomless basement to finally arrive at that 'foul rag and bone shop of the heart', as my all-time greatest poet, W.B. Yeats put it. And so it is with the songs on *Sex, Age and Death*, one of my two favourite records that I've made either with The Boomtown Rats or on my own. And I cannot listen to it.

I cannot listen to it not because it's bad but rather because it is too accurate and it is just too much for me. It may not be for anyone else, but I don't care. I can make sense of things by externalising sense. By writing them out of ourselves and being able to objectify stuff. Make it tangible and hold it out in front of ourselves and look at it, recognise it for the foul worm of despair that it is and say, "I know who and what you are, you fuck! Now. Get back into that dark and foetid hole you fester in."

Many of the images on this record just floated up out of the sump and I didn't argue. I tried to just, y'know, float. I had lost all control of my life, so just ... drifted. There's nothing else to do, so let it take you where you will end up anyway. A jellyfish. Insubstantial. Breathe in and then try to remember to breathe out again. That's the way. Time passes. The soul takes time to reassemble.

'Blow hateful wind/ Cold on faithless skin'. And then, from nowhere, 'Love will find a way to you again'. ('Blow Hateful Wind') It did. I was old now. But had never realised, till it was gone and found again that 'To live in Love is all there is/Life without Love is meaningless' ('To Live In Love'). It's absolutely true!!! What sort of a doofus was I? What sort of an eejit could invent their own life and not completely understand that there is but ONE absolute. It is only Love that makes life worth it. 'To live in Love/Is to Be'. The singular meta human characteristic is empathy. Without it we simply do not survive as a species. It is *why* we are so successful as a specimen of Evolution. Love is empathy exalted, being human in excelsis. Peak Personhood. The genius of the Beatles is again confirmed. All you actually *do* need is Love.

The album that followed *Sex, Age and Death* is called *How To Compose Popular Songs That Will Sell* and it is my other favourite. Equal and same. Bookends to horror and redemption. I can listen to this one. It has joy and gratitude and wonder. There would be more horror to come, but Love would assuage and share that and cast comfort upon the storm.

It's called *How To Compose Popular Songs That Will Sell* after a book I saw lying on my friend's piano. It was self-evidently an ironic title, as nobody by then was very much interested in my tunes any more, save for a good number of crazy Europeans who caught some virtue in them and had followed my course for years, thus allowing me my favourite thing to do. Go out, get on a stage and play these things. That is when they make sense. That is when it is no longer academic. That is where they jump out of their grooves or digital codes or off the page and live and breathe as wriggly, real, felt things. They make people dance! Isn't that mad? I write something in the kitchen one winter's February afternoon and you're leaping up, grabbing your girl, boy, partner and jumping around!! Or it makes you sad. Or happy. Or expresses what you think or feel but didn't quite know you did feel that or how to put into words... AND I DID THAT!!!!! So cool...

A Rose At Night

Here she comes like a Queen all through the wintertime
Skirts that billow long after she's gone
Yes I could smell her smell on the pillow late at night
She's a rose that blooms at night
And all the streets were wet and slicked with rain
Outside my green front door
Number 48 seemed dull by comparison
I went down to the pub to stock up for the long night by myself
That's one way out of this cold and lonely world
Yes I'll be a rose that blooms tonight

The city's quiet
The rioters have all gone home now
The fire brigades' sirens have been locked up for the night
There's a blackout down on Brown Street
Where all the blues come home
And yes there's a rose that blooms at night

See Jim he packed up all his bags and said
"It's time to get out of here"
But his wife and children they were crying out in the kitchen
Out in the back
Once a year he remembers that scene
But it seems so long ago now
He tries to remember more but he can't
You don't look back
Memories – they're like a rose that blooms at night

There's a clock that never strikes
In the Town Hall's towers of steel
There's a road that's never used
That's never kissed with the hiss of wheel
In your mouth is a rusted brace
That you flash in your junkyard smile
Shine on like a rose at night

BOB GELDOF

A Second Time

Alright I'm leaving
Why can't you stop crying
I won't take that blackmail
It's worse than your lying
It's worse than anything
You've ever done
But it's water off this ducks back
In the long run

And we can try an' work it out a little later
See if it's worth a second time around
Walk on the wild side but the right side
Yeah good luck, good luck from this boy
This next sad boy
Who's sitting here
Wishing you,
Wishing all goodbye

It's no use pretending
I think we got caught
We didn't need each other now
As much as we thought
And hey little sleepy girl
Wipe the wet from your eye
Time the Great Leveller
Should hold some surprise

And we can try an' work it out a little later…

A Sex Thing

Like the man who stands behind the man
And whispers in his ear
"Pretend you know the secret and then
Keep all your enemies near"
Well I held you close
And I squeezed so hard
It made your eardrums pop
But you hung there like a lifeless doll
And said I wonder could you ever stop

So what can I have if I can't have ermine
What can I have if I can't have pearls
Tell me what I need and then give it to me darling
But all I really want is your love baby

The hearts they bang like doors all night
And the shutters slam like cells
And the yellow rose of electricity blooms
And then flickers as someone yells
Well I heard that scream from far away
But it seemed so awfully near
Until I heard the sound of my own voice
Stinging in my ear

It said what can I have if I can't have ermine
What can I have if I can't have pearls
Tell me what I need and then give it to me darling
But all I really want is your love baby

I call you in the morning
And I call you in the night
And I call you in the early dawn
And the next time that I call you babe
I'll be calling long before you're born
Well the crows beat high
But they caw so clear
Like the croak of a dying man
Then they fall like an angry cloud to feed

BOB GELDOF

On the stooped and stunted corn
So what can I have if I can't have ermine
What can I have if I can't have pearls
Tell me what I need and then give it to me darling
But all I really want is your love baby

Do you take me for a fool
Do you take me for a wretch
When you take me for a little ride
But I'll take you in the morning
And I'll take you in the night
And I'll take you over on your side
And I'll take you in the front
And I'll take you in the back
And I'll take you in the middle too
But I wish you'd take me where I wanted to go
And I wish you'd come along too

It's just a sex thing
And that's enough
But I can't help it
If I fall in love

A Storm Breaks

A storm breaks over our head
We take shelter
We do as we're told

A storm breaks over our head
We take shelter
Come in from the cold

Life's OK
If you drink
Oh

Life's OK
If you dream
Oh

I can hear it
I can feel it
All around the air is freezing
Ice cold
(Ice cold, freezing cold)

Across the sea
Across the sky
Ice and Fire
Ice and Fire
So blow your
Breath into your hands
And wipe the frost
Out of yours

Life's OK
If you don't think
Oh

Life's OK
If you drink
Oh

A Summer Day – London '05

I've never seen the place look greener
Someone said it was the hottest year
Everything evaporating into
The cool high of the sky
Maybe the seas will boil up
Like the streets are now
Like a high fever
Like a high fever
The mercury will rise

Traffic snarls up from Oxford Street to the river
I've never seen it so low
Everybody lose their temper
Everybody got a gun
Loosen off a few shots
At the indifferent moon
At the pitiless sun

When suddenly
Through the grass
A cooling breeze
Comes to pass

Against The Whole World

Momma doesn't like me
And Daddy says "No"!
Your brother doesn't give a shit
And your Granny said "GO"!
So go pack your bags
I gotta £20 quid note
We're gonna get outta here
We're gonna go clear
There's no plan man
We're catching Life by the throat

Cos it's you and me
Against the whole fucking world

I got no shoes on
I got nothing in my head
I got nothing in my pocket
Man I just got outta bed
So I made a cup of coffee
Some toast and an egg
I'm just standing here watching
You sleeping in my bed

It's you and me
Against the whole fucking world

BOB GELDOF

An Icicle In The Sun

I know you're pretty and you're young
You're like an icicle in the sun
You sparkle and you shine okay
And one day soon you'll melt away
Fade away, melt away

It's six o'clock and growing colder
A woman looks out on the bay
Her breath is fogging up the window
But I could see her cry
The water glistened in her eye
It trickled down and caught the light
Then crashed down quietly

Yeah you're pretty and you're young
But no one said it's any fun
I know you heard somebody say
Every dog must have its day
It's not your day so bark away

It's eight o'clock and growing older
She wonders why they stay away
Her dress don't fit her like it used to
The meter's running out
She gets another shilling out
She sighs and then she settles down
Another evening

Yeah you're pretty and you're young
You're bursting out and having fun
From where I stand you look okay
Oh, I'll remember you this way
Come this way, don't delay

Play the worn-out tape
The one that has you smiling
Play the part where each one leaves
and waves goodbye
Turn the volume down
On all the old excuses
The ones that said I do
Or I will if I could it's true
'cause when you're old there's nothing new
But just remember

When you're pretty and you're young
It's sad to see what she's become
And you just wanna shake and shout
Meet somebody, going out
Look straight ahead and part the crowd
That covers her up like a shroud
You're know you're pretty and you're young
You're like an icicle in the sun
Number one rule of thumb

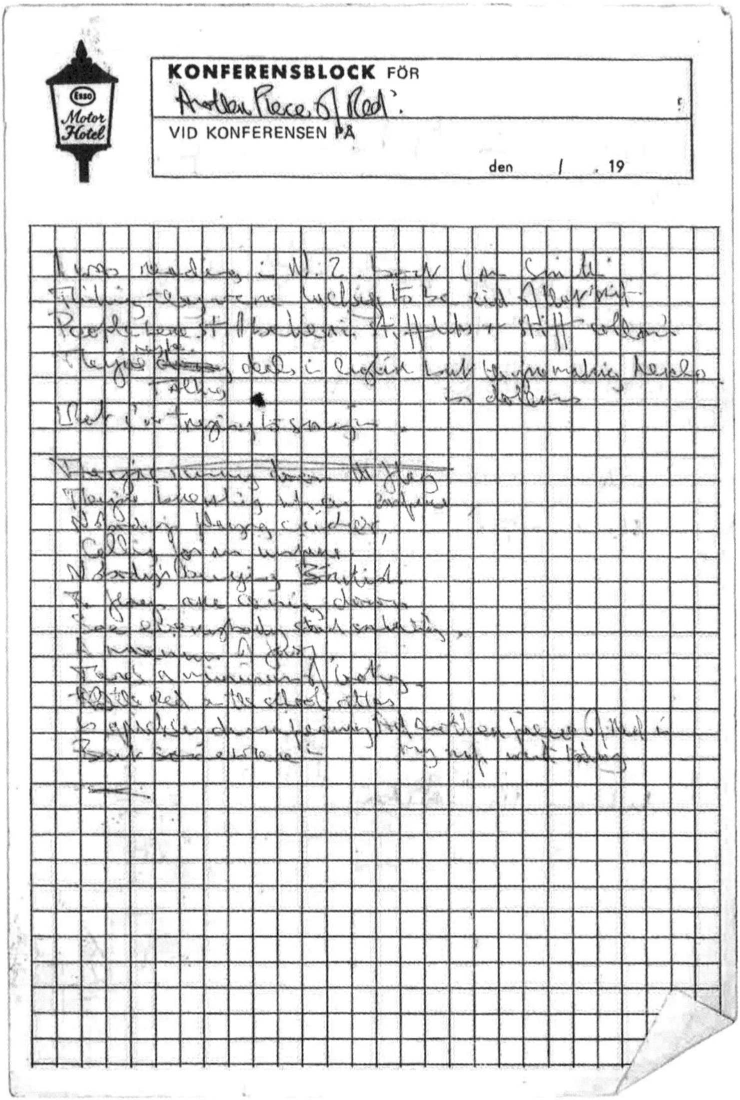

 'ANOTHER PIECE OF RED' DRAFT OF LYRICS

Another Piece of Red

Now we're in New Zealand. So oddly English. Home Counties cum Antarctica. In Australia they'd asked me whether they should become a republic. In India they were re-naming their cities from their anglicised versions. I kept saying Bombay and kept getting corrected. Then I read that Rhodesia was becoming Zimbabwe and that the arch-apartheidist leader of Rhodesia had fallen. I was happy. I had been involved with Anti-Apartheid since I was 13. Neither I, nor anyone else, foresaw that his replacement, once heroic, would become the mass murderous thug, Mugabe. That and the ruin of that glorious country was yet to come.

But what was forcibly striking was that we were walking, or in our case touring, through the last remnants of the British Empire. That 1950's schooltime when the geography maps coloured half the world in the pinkish-red of ownership and nobody thought it odd, was over.

BOB GELDOF

Another Piece Of Red

I was reading in New Zealand about Ian Smith
I was thinking they were lucky to be rid of that shit.
The people here can still believe in stiff lips and stiff collars
They're speaking deals in English
But they're making deals in dollars.
They're breaking up an empire
Nobody's buying British
They're calling for an umpire
Nobody's playing cricket
The flags are coming down and everybody stands saluting
But somewhere in the distance, I can hear somebody shooting.
And another piece of red left my atlas today.

It's so long Hong Kong
And no more Singapore
Those steaming nights of Malta
Goodbye Gibraltar
I'll give you arms for Africa
I'm hungry for India
The sun's set on Australia
And vive le Canada

They're breaking up an empire
Nobody's buying British
Calling for an umpire
It really isn't cricket
The flags are coming down
There's a minimum of looting
Somewhere in the distance I can see somebody shooting
And another piece of red left my atlas today...

MONDO BONGO, 1981

Attitude Chicken

We just couldn't believe our luck. The Wall collapsed just like that. The politicians all claimed ideological victory and swanked about in a misbegotten triumphalist glow. It could only have been down to the great genius of yer Reagans and yer Thatchers. This is nonsense, of course. It was just that the Soviets and their rubbish economy were broke and had been for years. I've quoted E.O. Wilson in another of these 'notes', but it's worth repeating his pithy summation of that particular theory of misunderstanding humanity; Communism. Great theory. Wrong species. Still, a different philosopher hubristically proclaimed the inevitable triumph of the Liberal Democratic order and signalled it as The End Of History. But I was more right when I wrote 'History never ends/It's too busy beginning' ('Roads Of Germany').

There are times when History is upon us. With luck, we have amongst ourselves elegant men and women who have the necessary humility and understanding to negotiate with the moment, rather than confront it and be defeated. A great bleeding is avoided. At those moments, men like de Klerk, Trimble and Gorbachev *et al.* attain nobility and the gratitude of a nervous world.

The effect on us was weird. A sort of vulgar triumphalism took hold, along with a strange new internalised politics. Not having an obviously visible enemy any longer, what was it we could define ourselves against? We were discomfited and discombobulated in such a strange, shapeless universe. Who now could we point the missiles at – that metaphorical finger-pointing thing? Indeed, what was the point in having all those guns and stuff any longer? Everyone was our mate now. This clearly wouldn't do.

Between then and now the world wobbled a bit. A strange vacuum of having no-one to be scared of or hate confused us. No need to freak out though. Everything would soon revert to biz as usual. Them pesky Arabs would soon come along (phew!), and Putin would pop up and put Russia back on its old inferiority-complex track and naked chest-beating (literally, in Putin's case), to the relief of politicos and their 'military/industrial' sidekicks. And hey wow, China – they're really coming up fast on the inside track and dude we can seriously be scared, thank god for those mothers. Yer Chinese don't mess around, they are seriously smart. So y'know, everything's back to normal now.

But between the ol' them 'n' us merry-go-round we beat ourselves up. We could turn in upon ourselves. Language and attitudes expressed through language came under attack. The 'meaning' of what one said needed to be 'deconstructed' to understand what someone *really* meant, even if what they meant was quite clear and as intended. Because, y'see, that clarity REALLY actually meant something else if you just drilled down into the actual language used, which would reveal one's true motivation for saying it in the first place! See? Words suddenly did not mean what you thought they meant.

I was in a diner in New York. In a booth. I was with Wally Meyerowitz. Y'know, *'Noo Yawk!'* Wally stared at the menu. It told us of the many offerings available and underneath the fancy names was a lavish and luridly purple description of how the dish would be prepared, cooked and how and what it would be served with. *'Nestling on beds of crystalline gem greens from the lushest fields of the Sonoma Valley, lovingly tended by caring hands of...'* bollox.

"Hi you guys. You still werkin' that card? Hokaaay. My name is Perky and I'll be yer table captain fer today. Back o' the ranch in the engine room we got Ralph who'll be fixin' up yer feud fer today. So whaddwe recknin' guys, ennythin' we ken help you with today?"

Wally scowls at the menu. He reads the elaborate description of what is basically a piece of poultry, looks up at Perky and says, "Yeah Perky, what da fock is dis attitood chicken?"

He was 100% hilarious and right. Language had lost its moorings. Words had become hopelessly adrift on an ocean of nonsense. People were being 'deeply hurt' by an assumed offence and a fresh minted hyper sensitivity to pico fractions of imagined identity slight. The highest of dudgeon received the warmest peer approval. Everyone could be a victim whilst victimhood was of great social benefit. The refusal to consider, never mind actually hear or listen to another's opinion (other than what ordained to be acceptable by an imposed 'groupthink') constitutes nothing less the shutting down of the critically objective mind. Voluntary intellectual abnegation is as abhorrent and dangerous to ourselves as any notional missile pointing at us, because it allows the actual awful grievances of the world to be ignored in an orgy of self-righteous indignation of the politically personal. Political correctitude is a sham and a dangerous farce. There are no 'safe spaces'. It's called Life. Get one.

Attitude Chicken.

Attitude Chicken

Later on that evening when
I thought I'd had enough
I sat down in a restaurant and
Over powdered drugs
I ordered up some dew-soaked lettuce
Picked by virgin hands
Nestling on a bed of
Pearl encrusted clams
Well the waiter's name was Renee and
He told me how his aunt
Who had 47 children
And how they'd always planned
To grow the smallest vegetables in
All the kingdom's land
"They're poor," he said "but happy and
Well that's what really counts"
And every evening after
Their 20 hour day
They'd sleep content imagining
That restaurant far away
Where fat fucks in designer suits
Would order over deals
The smallest portions of these
Tiny morsels for their meals

Still the blood it clots
And the hearts get stricken
See everybody's searching for... that attitude chicken

My Porsche got stuck in traffic and
My girlfriend said get real
How dare you get me stuck here
How d'you think that made me feel
I got a Yamaha 5 Million
A bike was what I needed
With my name spelt on the number plate
Like Paul Revere on speed
Yes my girlfriend's name is Anne

But she says the K is silent
Put the H after the A or
She gets "rilly violent"
She wears designer jewels
And she's got designer clothes
Which go with her designer mouth
Eyes, ass, tits and nose

And she does another line
And she's talking finger lickin'
And that's my signal to send out for...
that attitude chicken

A special breed
That fills the need
Is bred to feed
The endless greed
Yes it's poultry time
For all you little kittens
Let's get hip and do... attitude chicken

Now when she comes she screams designer screams
At precisely the right moment
Loud enough so the neighbours hear
And think I'm really potent
She's considerate like that
Which is why I guess I love her
And by that I hope you don't think
That I am trying to smother
Her uniqueness or her freedom
To find some other lovers
And express herself sexually
In attempting to discover
The inner self that every modern woman
In the land
Has a democratic right to
Which I as modern man
Of course respect and understand
And indeed can empathise with
Appreciate, articulate

Feel for and sympathise with
And any reference I might make
To her sexually
Has been vetted and approved of
By the Woman's Commissary

Still the plans get hatched
And the plots they thicken
See everybody's looking for... that attitude chicken

Neatly packaged politics
For all the little minds
It's the special interest lobby
For these multi-cultured times
The Politically Correct
Are the Nazis of our time
When it's the freedom of ideas
That makes man civilised.
Let's drag out the old scapegoat
If he's still alive and kicking
And go riding off in glory for that... attitude chicken

Gobble, gobble, gobble, gobble
Cluck, cluck, cluck, cluck
Attitude chicken
"I'd rather be a hammer than a nail"

BOB GELDOF

August Was A Heavy Month

I'll take another photograph
Before the old one fades
It reminds me of those things that passed
And quickly died away
But it comes on in the early night
Creeping up on you
Those scenes of devastation
Still crushing down on cue
The days are growing colder now
The light is growing dim
August was a heavy month
And now the nights are drawing in

Poor Baby Blue's wrapped up again
Inside her final pain
I'd help her if I could I say
She puts us all to shame
Alright, alright I know I've got a lot
Left to answer for
But am I the only one to blame
And anyway who's keeping score
But the grass seems so much brighter now
She's spilled her blood again
August was a heavy month
Wash it down September rain

Baby Blue picks up her life tonight
And rushes for the Chelsea train
All the stars shine down on her tonight
And August was a heavy month

The photograph is cracked and torn
From being picked up, put down
Like some holy relic
Whose worshippers are found
Searching through their sacred books
For the holy grail of "why"

But the sum of human knowledge
Knows no more than you or I
Alright, alright, says Baby Blue
Who doesn't really understand
August was a heavy month
But winter came at last.

Baby Blue picks up her life tonight
And rushes for the Chelsea train
All the stars shine down on her tonight
And August was a heavy month

BOB GELDOF

Baby's Going Down

Baby's going down again
She doesn't know it's time again
She never knows when it's over
She doesn't know when it ends
So Baby's going down again

But Baby says she's fine again
It just took a little time
This time again

The parties all swing around her
The darkness, her old dearest friend
Til Baby's going down once again

She said love is for wrestlers
Then threw me back down on the floor
and Baby's going down again

Baby says she's mine again
She says she wants to try again
So Baby's going down
Once again

Back To Boomtown

Calling...
In my head its calling
Then all the exile years will fall away

Its insistent
And Lord there's no resisting
You can twist and turn
But you can never turn away

I can pick your face out in a crowd
See your shape in every passing cloud
But Lord when you'd call my name
I used to feel ashamed
So tonight for just one night
I'm going to take that plane
That's bringing me
Back to Boomtown
...In my head

See it's bleeding
Boomtown's lying bleeding
It felt the sun for a second shine down upon its face
And then the rains came
Lord the heavy rain came
Now the sun won't shine on Billy's face again
Did you wake up from the stolen dream
To find yourself inside some nightmare scene
The streets like trees stripped bare
The empty houses stare
While the thieves and the liars of the night
Sneak away to steal
Somewhere else

I'm going
Back to Boomtown
In my head

Banana Republic,
This septic isle
This Judas in the sea,
I can't turn a blind eye,
When the blind can see.
I don't believe you,
You have nothing to say,
Your lies don't deceive me,
I.R.U.S.A.
You kill me,
Your ignorance is so complete,
They'll kill you,
With murder and deceit.
Banana Republic,
Septic isle.
Following me,
Police and priests
In the streets
~~Black belted gumbo~~
Hand in glove
With the killer streak

Come me Tally man
Tally me banana,
3 dead, 4 ruined,
Holy & Abandoned.
~~I despise you.~~ I loathe you,
~~You make me sick~~ Psychotic, ~~Holy~~ Sad insane
I despise you Mad dogs should be put down.
I.R.U.D.A.
Banana Republic, The septic isle
Wallow in your stupidity
Revere your history idols.
Christ is just right for you.
He dies to save,
I've never heard anything so stupid
Who's safe in the grave?
Blood sacrifice
Holy mother church,
Hand in glove,
~~With~~ the killers amuck.
Police & Priests
in the street
Banana republic.
You sicken me.

Banana Republic

History in Ireland is a whore. She's up for grabs to be used in whichever way by anyone at any time.

We had started our world tour with a 'triumphant' return to our homeland. We had done it. We had got out and 'made it'. That was the triumph. We had done what we had said we would. And more. The tv host had asked disbelievingly, "Do you honestly think you'll make it with that racket?" Cue audience laughter. "Yes, and we'll be back in a year at Number 1!" Cue more hilarity. But there we were, one year later, almost exactly. The first Irish band to get to Number 1 in the UK Top 20. Now we came to lay that tribute before them.

But they told us to fuck off. Typical, it has to be said.

The Pope had just visited. The place went nuts. Pope-mania ruled. He told us we were holier than anyplace else in the entire planet, so there! Put that in yer feckin' pipes 'n' smoke it!! Boomtown Rats, how are yeh!! One holy, Catholic and fuckin' Apostolic Ireland FOREVER...

We were booked to play two nights at the racecourse in Dublin and more specifically in this huge, long, papal-coloured, yellow and white candy striped 'tent' that had been used by JP2 and his mob as an 'after show' type dressing room cum thang. We thought that was great and hilarious. Il Papa and Us. *There* was the divide between one Ireland and the emerging newer one.

Well, the older Ireland weren't having it and they banned the gigs from happening. Oh, of course they dreamt up all sorts of plausible sounding, public safety type reasons for stopping it, but the real reason was there was no way that this bunch of foul-mouthed guttersnipes (i.e. Us) would ever blaspheme the blent, holy and possibly sacred feckin' air in which His Holiness had stripped down to his kacks.

We couldn't let them get away with it. We had to stay, and we *would* play! That was that. And the lines were set. We holed up in Blooms Hotel in central Dublin and were in and out of court. We lost every time. Police, insurance companies, judges and then the clergy, archbishops and politicians all joined in the fun and refused us anywhere to play. It wasn't a conspiracy, it was less obvious and more insidious than that, but no less subtle. We had pissed off too many people over those past two years with the things I'd said and the stuff we did and the obvious contempt we had for all of that crowd who had made Ireland into this shackled land of zero options. Ireland was a sham of a place. I had called it a 'banana republic. Guatemala towed into the north Atlantic'. And that was a gross disservice to that stricken country at that time.

No opportunity. A country that betrayed its young by offering no hope. A country of zero economy. A country whose political class were the apogee of cronyism and its attendant corruption. A land whose religious hierarchies held absolute sway over the morality AND the state, whilst many of its clergy and bishops quietly physically and sexually abused the children of their parishioners. An island embroiled in a murderous civil war that hardly merited comment whilst 3,600 people were killed, murdered, maimed or tortured. And a sanctimonious business class who were silent also cos they were far too busy raking their margins off the slagheap of state and religion to speak up. Though none of them appeared to even want to.

And us too. We were silent. Why? Why were we? I don't know is the answer. Maybe we had been taught to be silent. To bear our moral learned helplessness and economic impoverishment in holy silence. To bear our suffering with grace, for after all wasn't pain cleansing and our sinful selves didn't deserve anything more. Oh, you agents of sickening religious indoctrination and deception. You foul and holy liars. We fed ourselves on fantasy and distracted ourselves with inward looking shite and self-flagellation. A great silence reigned. A culture of being mute. A claustrophobia of silence. The great smothering of youth and hope and expectation. Well... fuck that.

The Boomtown Rats had other plans. Silence wasn't on the agenda. Noisome, irritating non-co-operation with the prevailing orthodoxies of the day seemed the right way to go. Self-aggrandisement rather than self-flagellation suited us nicely, thank you.

And so, when the time came, they got us. Nothing planned. We just sort of fell into their lap.

We stayed and fought and ultimately found a way around them. Outside their system, as ever. All secret until it wasn't and the young, the new, the different, the other real Ireland emerged, travelling overnight in their thousands to celebrate *their* victory, their baptism and our delayed homecoming in a mad, riotous, tumultuous gig in the grounds of an older, grander Ireland at the foot of an ancient castle.

Immediately after, I wrote the words of 'Banana Republic' in a state of deep bitterness. A brief de-coding; 'soldier's song' is the Irish national anthem. '40 shades of green' is the mawkish tribute to Ireland by Johnny Cash who mistakenly believed his ancestors came from there. Be led 'Up the garden path' is to be fooled. 'Police and Priests' I took from Junior Murvin's 'Police and Thieves' and maybe that's why the reggae beat was suggested. Pete wrote the brilliant descending bass line which suggested the music of the song. It's a light reggae pop song. If anyone knew the bitterness with which I wrote it or what I was on about, it probably wouldn't have been the hit it was. But we did that all the time. The object was to have hits. To change something, you must get inside it first. A musical variant on Trotskyite 'entryism'. We had to camouflage our way into the charts if people were to hear what we had to say. First an infectious tune then wrap it around the sense like a protective inoculating sheath. A musical prophylactic. An innocent enough little pop tune then maybe a while later someone would be humming it to themselves and they'd go, "Oh... yeah... of course."

The band never really knew what the words were. They didn't care. And it didn't bother me, and they never asked, and I never told them what the words were or what I thought a song was about. But weirdly they got the sense and feel of something and could propel the song to its intended destination.

Same with the song I described above, 'Elephant's Graveyard' or 'I Don't Like Mondays' or 'Rat Trap' or many others. Doesn't really matter if you get it or not. You'll take what you want from it anyway. But for me, there was always the satisfaction of knowing that if it was a hit then there's a thing out there worming its way through somebody's brain.

Though, 'She loves you, yeah, yeah, yeah,' works equally for me. In fact, that's where real pop-writing skill lies. Now *that's* something I wish I could do.

Banana Republic

Banana republic
Septic Isle
Screaming in the suffering sea
It sounds like dying
Everywhere I go
Everywhere I see
The black and blue uniforms
Police and priests

And I wonder do you wonder
While you're sleeping with your whore
That sharing beds with history
Is like a-licking running sores
Forty shades of green yeah
Sixty shades of red
Heroes going cheap these days
Price; a bullet in the head

Banana Republic...

I'll take your hand and lead you
Up the garden path
Let me stand aside here
And watch you pass
You're striking up "A Soldier's Song"
I know that tune
It begs too many questions
And answers to,

Banana Republic...

The purple and the pinstripe
Mutely shake their heads
A silence shrieking volumes
A violence worse than they condemn
Stab you in the back yeah
Laugh into your face
Glad to see the place again
It's a pity nothing's changed

Banana Republic...

BOB GELDOF

The Banker's Song

The bankers gone and stolen all my money
The bankers gone and lost all of my dough
He robbed my pension fund from out of my old age
My children's education, food and home

The banker says he can't lend me no money
The money's disappeared there's none to loan us
He said he shared my fear about our future
He's lost his job and half a millions bonus

The banks have gone and gambled all my money
They've broke our countries back and me as well
If I'd have done what you have done I bet you
I'd rot for years inside some jailhouse cell

Yeah the government said they'd end all unemployment
Endless growth was the new paradigm
An end to boom and bust and new depressions
Hey buddy can you spare me some old dime

That's right

Those fucking bankers!

Battersea Morning

Battersea Morning
It's bright in the early dawning
The little birdies sing to me
From the trees

And I've got a new bike
It's just like my old bike
But when I ride it I feel nice
On those Battersea mornings

The city is waiting for me
It's always there waiting for me
I go there and I see my friends
You should see us go crazy

On Battersea mornings
Going shopping without warning
We go cycling through the park
We get healthy
Unlike the rest of the week

Battersea morning cross the bridge in those early dawnings
The river sliding by beneath
My 5-speed wheels yeah

BOB GELDOF

The Beat Of The Night

It was cold that night
When the crows flew west
And the days had lost their spark
And the yellow light
Split the rain soaked night
And the dogs forgot to bark
What Hitchcock plots
Were hatched that night
Behind the shuttered doors
When a curtain shook
And a head peeped out
Then quietly was withdrawn
As we moved in the beat
The beat of the night

So I made my way
To the top of the hill
And I looked on down the road
And the air stood still
In the frost and chill
As the hours and the minutes unfold
But the trees they shook
And the houses creaked
As though seized by a violent rage
And the wind bites deep
And the wires shriek
Like a noise from beyond the grave
And we moved in the beat
Swayed in the beat
The beat of the night

The sound of women crying
Made me go and investigate
So I walked past a row of houses
Till I reached number 48
Where the huddled neighbours stood about
Frightened, shocked and scared
And then the bleating of an ambulance

Cut through the thickening air
With a sickening sense of déjà vu
I knew what was coming next
I'd been here before
But when or how
I couldn't quite connect
Then from an open windowed upstairs flat
Someone sang along
Yes I knew the words
And I knew the tune
They were playing a Beatles song
That went
Yeah, yeah, yeah

A black man slumped up against the door
A brown man lay face down on the floor
A white woman sobbed on the second stair
And all the blood was red
And we moved in the beat
The beat of the night

Yes the tears of rage
And the tears of anger
Flow to the river bank
And at the local disco dance hall
They were cranking up the skank
And the pulse of that noise cut through the night
Until it washed up at my feet
And I smelt the fear
And I tasted blood
And the soundtrack was the beat
The beat of the night.

BOB GELDOF

Before The Day Begins

Before the day begins
I lie awake
Before the day begins
The snake that sheds
It's too worn skin
I start again
Before each day begins

Before the day begins
The dawn allows
The light seep in
That sickly greyish dim
And so each day begins

And as each day begins
The world seems thin
Between my bones and skin
This flimsy thing
I live within
Breathing out
Then breathing in
Remembering to live

Before the day begins
The planet does
Its daily thing
Like us it will
Rotate and spin
We too thought
That we could win
But knew the night
Would claim us too

Before the daily dawn
I watch you stir and yawn
A thousand mornings
Been and gone
Another day begins

Big Romantic Stuff

Did they never tell you 'bout it baby
Did they never say it's tough
Are you never going to give up on that
Big romantic stuff

That French song playing on the radio at noon
The singer's name was Jean Michel and he's singing
'bout la lune
And she shivers as she comes awake
And remembers how to think
And she shakes the hair out of her eyes
But the daylight makes her blink
And the song it whispers in her mind
like a half-forgotten sigh
Of times of love, the longest days
And youth and endless skies
And ooh la la la
Did they never tell you 'bout it baby
Did they never say it's tough
Are you never going to give up on that
Big romantic stuff

To ease the pain of it, to fill the empty void
She stores up ancient souvenirs like ravens with their hoards
It's not the getting old she minds
It's the meaningless of being
She thinks about all this while
Jean sings about la vie
And accordions and violins take her back in time
When the only explanation was a kiss and love and life

BOB GELDOF

The Bitter End

To the bitter end
We go all the way
It isn't too far
It isn't too far

To the bitter end
With our wills of iron
Souls of coal
Hearts of gold

To the bitter end
Sit on a fence all day
Looking for change
Any spare change

To the bitter end
And on the side that wins
How can you lose?
We always do

To the bitter end
When the wind bites cold
Look at the rain
England in May

To the bitter end
We'll go all the way
It isn't too far

And it goes on

Blind Date

On blind dates
You meet in corners,
You take a jump into the unknown,
They're classified,
They're top secret,
An antidote to being on your own.

You're standing waiting,
You're hesitating,
You're thinking maybe... well
I don't know
Your nerve is breaking,
You've started praying,
But you're still staying...
And you don't know for what
But I still say
I've been alone too long
And been alone's so wrong
I've been alone too long.

A blind date's
A blinkered meeting
A rendezvous with some person unknown,
A secret tryst, a shady dealing,
A gamblers chance when loves dice are thrown.

But you've checked the classifieds in all the papers,
And you've filled in all your forms and tried Computadata
See ya later
What a waste of a
Blind date...

BOB GELDOF

Blow Hateful Wind

Blow hateful wind
Cold on faithless skin
Higher than the highest high
Love will find a way to you again

Flow bitter seas
Thrown down on buckled knees
Colder than the oldest sin
Love will find a way to you again

Can you speak it
Yes I'll speak of thin, bleak Winter moons
Will you speak it
Yes to boneless ghosts of empty rooms
And repeat it
Yes to maddened priests of waste and ruin
But love will find a way to you again

Blow hateful wind

Love will find a way to you again

Blowfish

I been drinking like a blowfish
Drinking 'til my throat is dry
I been drinking like a blowfish
Drinking 'til my mouth is dry
If I drink enough already
Lord I won't ever hear you cry

I been eating like a monkfish
Cos my stomach's got a hole
I been eating like some monkfish
Just a little feeds my soul
Yeah I been gnawing like a dogfish
Chewing on that cancer bone

You're sick and tired of me baby
I can't even stand myself
You're sick and tired of me baby
I can't stand it myself
You see the monkfish took my halo
And the blowfish took my breath

BOB GELDOF

Blue Balloons

Too cruel to be true
Those dreams they had for you
They blew them up
They flew away
In blue balloons

And now there's no-one there
A vacant bed or chair
Fills up the empty air
That leaks from blue balloons

I don't know how I get through these days he says
I don't know how I get through these days she says

And in that hollow space
Where once they saw your face
That bitter void replaced
By smirking blue balloons

I don't know how I get through these days he says
I don't know how I get through these days she says

Too cruel to be true
Those dreams they had for you
They blew them up
They flew away
In blue balloons

The Boomtown Rats

Around us in that dank, dark, hopeless Dublin of 1975, Ireland sank into a stupor of what was in effect civil war. Not the euphemistic 'Troubles', so often used to refer to the killing and murder of 3,600 people. As though we were suffering from nothing more than a small bout of political flu. We got so used to what was happening 80 miles up the road it had become the corruptive norm. We didn't really care. Didn't give a shite. Bloody Sunday sickened us alright and we enragedly erupted. But then a sort of supine indifference glazed over us once more. A particularly egregious outrage/episode/murder would make the front page, but yer basic common or garden murder barely merited a couple of paragraphs.

We ALL knew what the soon-to-be Prime Minister and his fellow-traveller cronyists were up to in their silent, implied and often explicit support of one side or another. Not just moral support, but many of the government overtly colluded with funds, arms, diplomatic support whilst of course presiding over an, as ever, disabled and moribund economy that allowed no future for its young. They were all a treasonous disgrace. There is an expression in Ireland: "Oh he's a cute whore alright." It's an expression of implied admiration and approval to one who is sharp. Sharp practice. Smart. It's said with a wink. "Oh he's a cute hoo-er alright." Wink. No flies on him/her. "Wudja ever give it a rest, Geldof? Shir you'd do the same if you had the chance." No I wouldn't. "Ah would you ever fuck off, shir he's one cute hoo-er is Charlie." Wink. Yes, he was. We were all living under The Cute Whoredon of Charles J. Haughey, Taoiseach Na hÉireann.

The All Powerful One Holy Catholic and Apostolic Church – save for a very, very few hardy priests – stayed hypocritically silent on the murders. And on the appalling social conditions of many. Of course they did. They were far too busy 'giving guidance' as to the moral character and tone of their constituents whilst busily fucking the children of their parishioners. Still we were silent.

As for the 'business' class, they got their illegal 'development' lands from their 'friends' in government, dodgy loans from their mates in the crooked banks, nudged and winked alongside all the above vis-a-vis the killers in the North (and sometimes South) and generally puked with impunity down upon the people and the country. Cute whores all. And we knew it all and still were silent.

A terrible claustrophobia of silence smothered us. A great holding-in of national breath. A suffocating political/economic/moral bubble vacuum. It had to give. It had to go. We had to breathe. Fuck silence! The Boomtown Rats had a clear intent and purpose. More than a band, they were an idea. And they were not silent. They were very noisy indeed.

And there was a reason. Like any other band we had tried a couple of names for ourselves, tried rolling them around our tongue. Tried to be whatever the name was. But we just weren't whatever the name that week was. Then, mystically enough, on the night before our first gig the stars aligned, the cosmic chorus hummed its secret chord and I began to re-read Woody Guthrie's biography, 'Bound For Glory', and came across our name. The Boomtown Rats.

Bob Dylan had led me to Woody, as Mick and Keith had told me to listen to Lightning, Howlin' and Muddy. Were these forces of nature or men? Well both, actually. The names alone compelled a listen. What did a Blind Lemon look like? When I heard him, I knew. And then the others. Robert, John Lee, Skip, Mississippi John – all sublime in their perfect primitive sophistication and all for some bizarre reason knew exactly how I felt. But forces of nature they were. They hit me hard, those men and that music. All true. Every gut-wrenching note.

Briefly, Woody Guthrie travelled and lived and worked amongst the poor and homeless of the American Depression. He wrote songs about these people. They are simple, timeless, angry songs in which the people could recognize themselves within them and would sing them in the hobo camps of 1920/30s America. But they were so good, these songs, they outlasted their moment. Their anger and simplicity and truthfulness were timeless, so that his most famous tune of all became the alternative national anthem of the US. Sung, no less (and triumphantly so), at the official formal inauguration of the 44th President. It is a devastatingly simple, beautiful song. 'This Land Is My Land' is about simultaneous ownership and dispossession and is full of beauty and a calm, dispassionate rage against injustice.

I was 15, working at night with a crowd in Dublin who gave food and shelter to that city's dispossessed. Broken people, hookers, bag ladies and the lost and the hopeless, homeless, etc. Through those cold nights around a big fire in Smithfield I thought I was living those songs. I wasn't of course, I was going home to a cold but comfy bed. I was fed. I was in school. But it made me boil as only the adolescent can boil in the pure heat of unmediated passionate rage, and both Dylan and his mentor spoke to everything I felt.

Guthrie lived in a small town where they had found oil. New kids arrived with the oilmen and their families. 'Boomchasers.' Woody was part of the local kids' gang who refused entry to the new kids on the basis that they 'didn't belong'. In disgust, young Woody left and started his own gang, only admitting the new kids. A sneering old gang member spat an insult at this new crowd of kids who wanted nothing to do with the old gang. "...Y'ore pack of mangy curs! Boomtown Rats!!!" Yea fucking sure we didn't belong. Fucking sure we were angry. Fucking absolutely 100% we didn't want to be part of the old, moribund, redundant gang and fucking sure things round here needed to change. Mangy curs we were. Boomtown Rats we ARE. And so it was. It FELT exactly right.

Rock 'n' roll has always been an avatar of change for me. A type of musical activism. When things were less than wonderful as a child, when things were dark, hemmed in and hopeless, then a thin gold thread dangled out of the magnetic purple ether and through the radiogram each night. And oh, I grabbed hold of it with a fierce intensity that has not slackened since. It emerged from the improbable microstate of Luxembourg via the one pop station in the UK and Ireland. From this mad broadcasting confection emerged all the ideas of my time through the voices of the girls and boys with guitars. It spoke in that low time of whole other universes and possibilities. It demanded the change that was not only inevitable but the desirability and necessity of that change itself. Pop itself was the rhetoric of change and the music was and would be the platform for that change. I have been able to use that idea ever since, whether through the Rats or the solo songs or the Amnesty shows, the Sun City record, Band Aid, Live Aid, Live 8 and so on.

BOB GELDOF

The Boomtown Rats

I'm gonna Boomtown
I'm going back
Back to Boomtown
Yea that's where I'm at
And when I get to Boomtown
I'm gonna ask those cats
What's happening here in Boomtown?
"It's those Rats, those Rats
Those dirty Rats,
Those RrrrrrrrrrATS!

D'ja wanna come to Boomtown?
I'll meet you round the back
Between the dirty alley
And those Boomtown Flats
They're dedicated to St. Boomtown
He's the patron saint of crap
He's praying for a miracle
But what he gets is
Those Rats, those Rats
Those filthy Rats
The Boomtown Rats
(YEA!!!)
The Boomtown Rats
(MEGAAAA)

Born To Burn

Set the guitar control to stun
I wanna hear that tommy gun
Those power chords begin to churn
That band was born to burn

The drummers started firing
Keep your head way down low
The bass guitar is pumping
Man these walls are gonna blow
Piano players thumping keys
Ain't nothing they need learn
Cos there's nothing you can teach 'em
They were born to burn...

That's all I remember of this one. It's enough. You get the drift...

BOB GELDOF

The Bright Lights Of Dublin

The bright lights of Dublin are twinkling tonight
You can see them across Scotsman's Bay
And they gleam in the night
Like the glow of a promise
That disappears at the dawn of the day

All the talkers, the dreamers and would-be big hitters
The gobshites, the gougers and big time bullshitters
Conjure a life and hold up a bar
Or lie down in Wilde's gutters
Looking up at the stars

Ambition will rise in the gorge like a vomit
And drown in its own puke
Just as quick as a comet
I'd leave if I could and I'll go sometime soon
A pen in my coat and a pocket of tunes.

Can't Stop

Can't stop,
And face the facts.
Can't stop,
Can't stop now.
I'm highly strung and I can't relax.
Tune me down cause I'm feeling sharp.
Blood's too weak it strains my heart.

And hearts of gold can turn to grey,
And wills of iron can melt away.
Hey, this looks like the place.
We can stop, pick up some fame.

Can't stop
Oh doctor, please
I bruise so easy and I cut so clean
Cure me quick, bring me to my knees
Knock me out, come on I wanna sleep.

Doctor please, cure me quick.
Doctor please, I feel sick.
Doctor please, what's that pain.
Doctor please, here it comes again.

Can't stop
I can't slow down
My nose is bleeding, hanging upside down.
My head is reeling, I don't hear a sound
My mouth's dry, it turns me inside out.

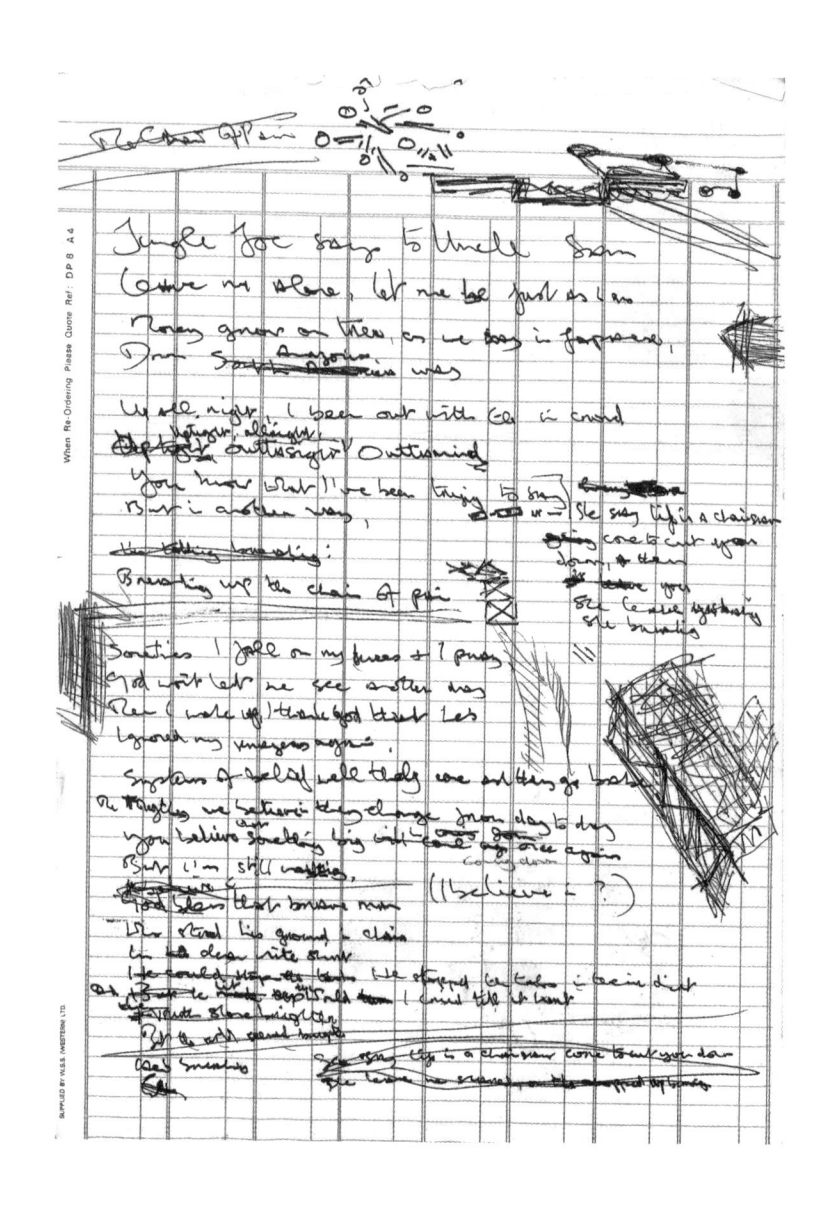

The Chains Of Pain

Jungle Joe say to Uncle Sam
He say leave me alone
Let me be just as I am
Money grow on tree
As we say in Japanese
Down Amazonia way
Up all night I've been out with the in crowd
Uptight, outtasight, alright, outtamind
You know what I'm trying to say
But in another way

And I'm not waiting
I'm breaking up the chains of pain
A chain that breaks is just a heart that's changed

Sometimes I fall on my knees and I pray
God won't let me see another day
Then I wake up and I thank God that He's
Ignored my prayers again
Systems of belief well they come and they go babe
The myths we believe in they change from day to day
I believe belief will wrap your brains in chains
So I'm for changing

Desperate deeds were done
By men with guns in China
Boys in clean white shirts
Stopped the tanks in their dirt
And the blood they spilled
Just made the white shine brighter
They weren't waiting baby
They were breaking up the chains of pain
They're not slaves they're changing
By breaking up the chains of pain
A brain in chains is just a heart enslaved
Join the chain gang
Break it up

BOB GELDOF

Charmed Lives

Charmed lives
Nothing much to do tonight
Charmed lives
Oh no, oh no
Charmed lives
I think I'll do my hair tonight
Charmed lives
Cos it's so, it's so

Well, it's OK,
But it drives me insane
Can't do a thing with it
Look at it
This way and that
Pile it up?
Spray it on?
Grease it straight back?

Charmed lives
Nothing much to do today
Oh no, oh no
Think I'll see some friends today
Cos they're so... they're so they're so...

Yeah they're OK,
And we all think the same
Cos we're on the phone
But hear the news
It's all grief and gloom
Yes things are bad
Really bad
But we're clearly immune
We lead
Charmed lives

Cheerio

We've been standing here five minutes
And you haven't said a word
Maybe you did
Maybe I haven't heard
You better hurry up
And say something
Or else I'm gonna go

Okay that's fine by me
Cheerio

BOB GELDOF

Close As You'll Ever Be

Down at the street around half past nine
I heard someone screaming
I found someone dying
His throat was slit from ear to ear
He mumbled so low I could hardly hear
I bent down low so I could hear what he said
He said tell me the truth am I nearly that dead
I said you're close as you'll ever be.

Down on the beach around half past five
I saw a pretty girl on a deck-chair reclining
A grin split her face from ear to ear
I went up close I must have got too near
Cos I never saw the guy on the sea-front café
Leaving his seat coming running my way
Saying you're close as you'll ever be
Oh yeah you're close as you'll ever be

Down at the car lot around half past five
I saw a cream coloured Cadillac I'd love to make it mine
It was chrome-plated shining silver bumper to rear
It must have done near a ton in only first gear
I asked for the gentleman in charge of sales
The dude left the office and came running my way
And he says you're as close as you'll ever be

Cool Blue And Easy

I got a little brittle heart
That's nothing new
Open up a window
Let the night breeze blow on through
Were you breathing?
It's cold

Brother, brother, brother
Here's something you should know
The birds will sing for summer
Like the wolves will howl for snow

Brother, brother, brother
Me, I long for the night
Cool, blue and easy
It's going to be alright

I stretch my hand and turn on the night
(cool, blue, easy)
I strike its black satin skin
I let it suffocate me

That same night
That night touches you
And at that moment of touching
It smothers you

Then I lick the night
And this exact same night washes you
Then I kiss the night goodnight
And this same night moves against you

The city whoops and shrieks
The traffics swish and hiss
Don't leave me with the quiet
I got nothing to fill it with

BOB GELDOF

Shake this town
Fill the void
Rattle them bones
With ambulance noise

Beaky Concorde throttles down
Shake it up
Shake this town

In the orange sodium glow
The drunkards streaming piss
And it's at times like this
And it's on nights like this...

In the overhead flats
They're busy watering plants
Threads of overflow
Indolent snot streams
Splash the flags

The non-stop fuck champions in the flats above
Are doing their thing
And then I know there's a God
I know there's a God

And I'm cool, blue
And I'm easy

Crazy

Here comes the night again, babe
Same night as every night, babe
And in the candle light, babe
Your beauty's like a knife
That slices through my life and

You drive me crazy
Makes my world fall apart
I've been trying lately
To take control of my heart

All days are good or bad days
But these days most days are bad days
And in this sacred place, babe
The days all fade away
When I see your face and

You drive me crazy
Makes my world fall apart
I've been trying lately
To take control of my heart

And when I saw you tonight
You know I almost died
I'd never seen anyone
Lovelier than you
As beautiful as you

BOB GELDOF

Crucified Me

First time that I saw you
You were standing in the hall
You said you knew everything
But I knew you knew fuck all
There were tremors in your cheekbones
There was longing in your eyes
But I thought I smelt a nameless fear
Buried in your thighs
You crucified me

Do you see
That you crucify me

I crouched down in the hallway
You huddled on the step
There were shadows in the alcove
We were way out of our depth
There was thunder in the hallway
There was lightning at the gate
Electric storms flashed through the walls
In fixed and fluid states
And crucified me.

Do you see
That you crucify me

Now and then I call your name
And now and then it's clear
Baby you can call in vain
Even though you're near
You were cloaked in your depression
Like a widow in her veils
How could we begin to think
That we could ever fail
You crucified me

First time that I saw you
You were standing 'gainst the wall
You swore I knew everything
But you knew I knew fuck all.

Dave

Dave was a year or two ahead of me in school. He lived in a big house, behind the trees on the acute turn the 7a had to make coming out of Blackrock around to Seapoint. Other than that, all I knew was his reputation for being out of it on Demerol cough medicine. Got so bad he'd get banned from successive pharmacies around the area and gradually need to make forays further afield to chemist shops that didn't know him. It ended up that he spent most of the day on public transport looking out for newer places to get his hit. I knew he could play though.

So, the years pass and *poco a poco* he gets to play with the Rats. He'd kicked the opioids but was into coke now. And there was enough of that around pop (and not that infrequently, us) to accommodate his naturally wired, taut persona. We told him if it affected his saxophone then he was out. Nothing but nothing interferes with the gig. All this was after a couple of shows where he couldn't control his manically working jaws long enough to fix his lips to the mouthpiece of his sax and burp a sort of liquid blubbering fart sound out of his horn. We made him a t-shirt with 'I fought the jaw and the jaw won' on it. Hilarious but y'know, get it together or fuck off.

Coming back from the North at night we dropped him on the nearest corner to his digs. He had a lovely girlfriend. She was dead in the toilet when he walked in. OD. A £5 bag of smack. I suppose the price doesn't matter. If it had been a £5 grand bag would that have been different? More worth it or something? No. It's just... a whole life... five quid... I don't know.

Now it's around 3am. I have long been home and I'm asleep in bed, and the phone goes. It's Dave and he is distraught. He is sobbing and in awful pain. I am half-asleep, trying to make sense of what he is trying to tell me. There is nothing to say. There never can be anything to say. Whatever I do say it is inadequate as it always must be. It is not a long conversation and I cannot go back to sleep. That morning I write what I perhaps should have said, but it doesn't matter because whatever *is* said will always go unheard. Nothing human can penetrate that inhuman grief.

It's a good song that one. I think I got the moment in that one. It came easy and it came true and it was effortless for the band to pick up on it and play it like it was meant to be played. Later, it was strange to play live with Dave himself doing some of the backing vocals. I never said anything about the tune to him and I don't think any of the others did. But he knew and therefore there was nothing further to be said or discussed.

'Dave' was the song that should have been a hit in 1984 but wasn't. This was the song that prefaced the end of phase 1 of the band, the one that signalled to us that the jig was probably up. I had naively believed that if a record was simply good enough then it would slide into the charts. But that's not so. Our time, it seemed, was coming to the end of its run. We were out of favour now. There were newer kids around with different ways of doing it and saying it and after 10 years radio was telling us the race was run. They wouldn't play it and we couldn't get it on TV. The Americans told me that I had to change the words because no station in the US would play a song of love from one man to another. "Yeah, okay cool, what do you want me to do?" Change the words? Okay. I'll call it 'Rain' and alter the first line and... I did but it made no difference...

I was frightened. I had never imagined The End. There were intimations it was coming. A glaring lack of interest in the current doings of the band from anyone. We could still sell out shows with the fans of the recent years but new stuff... nah. The Boomtown Rats... yawn. I mean intellectually I agree 'n' all but it's hard to stomach when it happens. What was I going to do now to keep house, home, partner and new baby going? Was the new album going to tank as well...?

I got home early and turned on the telly to watch the news. There was stuff about Africa...

'DAVE' EARLY DRAFT OF LYRICS

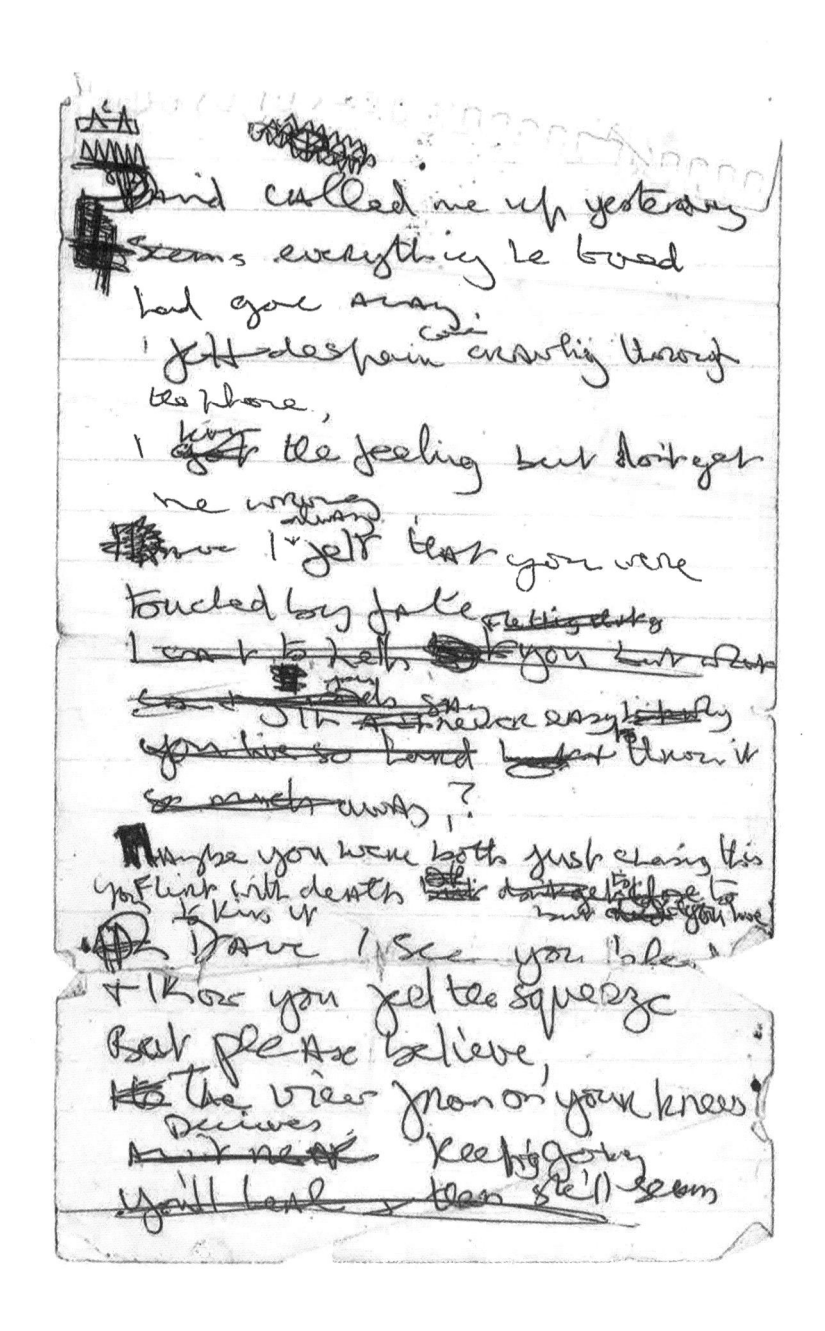

Dave

David called me up yesterday
Everything he loved had moved away
I felt despair come crawling through that phone
I know the feeling but don't get me wrong
Dave I've always felt that you were touched by fate
It's never easy but why throw it away?
Maybe you were both chasing this?
Flirt with Death but never kiss her.
Dave

I keep dreamin'
I'll set the scene,
So what's a fiver?
Why so mean?
The golden moment
The blinding gleam
It's all over
That's too cheap.
Dave

And Dave, I see you bleed
I know you feel the squeeze,
But please believe
The view from on your knees
Deceives
Keep going

I know you're empty
I know you're numb
And you can't function
I know that you're drunk
But Dave I've always felt
That you were touched by fate
The thing that gets me is the stupid waste
So pick it up and don't put it down
A newer story in another town

BOB GELDOF

I see you bleed
I know you feel the squeeze
Time heals
Believe
Then it will seem you dreamed
These things
Long ago
Dave

Keep going Dave

Dazzled By You

In abandoned empty rooms
Lying naked in my ruin
And I was dazzled by you
Dazzled by you

I was whipped and I was raw
When I looked up and I saw you
And I was dazzled by you.

I had barely survived
Saw no point in being alive
And I was dazzled by you

And with a cold and bitter venom
I hated each and every woman
But I was dazzled by you

In the midst of my despair
I was coming up for air
When I was dazzled by you

With your soft and tender touch
You gently picked me up
I was dazzled by you

BOB GELDOF

Deep In The Heart Of Nowhere

Hey baby there's a storm coming up
It's still about nine miles down range
Don't get excited
We're not hoping
Those winds are blowing up
The winds of change
But if you want me
You know where
I'll be waiting for you
If you need me
I'll be here
True blue
Deep in the heart of nowhere.

Diamond Smiles

"Traffic's wild tonight"
Diamond smiles her cocktail smile.
Tonight she's in heavy disguise.
She looks at her wrist to clock the passing time.

"Weather's mild tonight"
She wonders do they notice her eyes,
She wonders will her glamour survive,
And can they see she's going down a third time.

Everybody tries,
It's Dale Carnegie gone wild,
But Barbara Cartland's child
Long ago perfected the motionless glide.

In the low voltage noise,
Diamond seems so sure and so poised
She shimmers for the bright young boys,
And laugh's "Love is for others, but me – it destroys"

The girl in the cake
Jumped out too soon by mistake,
Somebody said the whole thing's half-baked
And Diamond lifts her glass and says "cheers"

She stands to one side
There's no more to this than meets the eye,
Everybody drinks Martini dry,
And talks about clothes and the latest styles.

They said she did it
With grace.
They said she did it
With style.

They said she did it all
Before she died
Oh I remember Diamond's smile

BOB GELDOF

Nobody saw her go,
They said they should have noticed
Cos her dress was cut so low.
Well it only goes to show
Ha, ha, how many "real men" any of us know.

She went up the stairs,
Stood up on the vanity chair,
Tied her lame belt around the chandelier,
And went out kicking at the perfumed air.

Dig A Ditch

When it gets to you
You gotta dig a ditch
When the war comes on
You gotta dig a ditch
And when the bills come in
You gotta dig a ditch
And the sky turns grey
You gotta dig a ditch
And it starts to rain
You gotta dig a ditch
And then you start to pray

When there's nothing left for me to do
I'm going to hold on tight to you
And as the world about us crumbles and falls
Then darling reach out and touch me

When it all dries up
Dig a ditch
And the trees drop down
Dig a ditch
And the seas dry up
Dig a ditch
And if you start to drown
Dig a ditch
And it's raining from a hole in the sky
And you can't look up
Case it burns your eyes
And they tell you that's the price you pay
Then darling reach out and touch me

Dig a ditch
When you hear the news
Dig a ditch
Hear those points of view
Cos I'm listening to some stupid twat
And he's trying to tell me
That he knows where it's at

When he couldn't find his ass in the bath
Then darling reach out and touch me

Dig a ditch
When you go insane
Dig a ditch
You won't feel the pain
Dig a ditch
When you're on the make
Dig a ditch
And you get a break
Dig a ditch
You don't feel the pain
Dig a ditch
You got it on your brain
Well I'll tell you what we're going to do
We'll build a cosy house here just for me and you
And in a cellar watch it all come down

Dig a ditch

When it all dries up
And the trees drop down
And the sea dries up
And you start to frown
And your mouth won't stop
And your eyes won't shut
And your arms don't swing
And your lips glued up
And your legs don't move
And your brain don't move
And your tongue don't move
And you're stuck in the groove
Stuck in the groove
Stuck in the groove
Stuck in the groove
Stuck in the groove
Stuck in the groove
Stuck in the groove
Stuck in the groove

Do The Rat

The first thing I did specifically for The Rats was a joke. It was however a joke with intent. It had a purpose.

Throughout the 50s, 60s and 70s the 'showbands' were an institution in Ireland. They were groups of players who went around the 'ballrooms' of the country bringing entertainment to these cavernous, alcohol-free, priest-ridden, cold halls in the pre-television age. They were decent enough players and it allowed musicians to at least earn a living from their work. Sort of up-scale wedding bands. But they were horribly hopeless also. Both bands and halls were tightly controlled by a small group of exploitative 'businessmen' in what was in effect a small-town type of Mafia. There are those apologists for this musical and exploitative corruption who say that at least there were some good musicians in there. Maybe, but so what? This had nothing to do with music. This was about everything else except music. It was by its very nature anti-music. Our view was that the showbands actually prevented people of proper talent from emerging. They were paid a small wage, they got their 6 Cavan Colas and 'hang samwidges' after the gig and they drove home from wherever. And that was enough. They could see no possibility of perhaps being original and joining in the revolution that was happening around the world in the 60s. That music could be ABOUT something. Could MEAN something. Could express things that otherwise were incapable of being articulated. And crucially they couldn't see that the TV age had made them horribly redundant. One or two twigged early that this was the road to musical perdition and got out. Van Morrison. Rory Gallagher and...?

For me, they were just one more example of the implicit corruption of the culture, economy and the institutions of the awful Church/State compact that was the Irish constitution and the original sin of the morass it inevitably led to. Indeed, one of the more notorious of the ballroom and showband owner/operators became the Irish Prime Minister. This was just one more simple manifestation of the Banana Republic that had to be broken. It had to change.

A lot of the showbands had their own dance. The most famous, 'The Hucklebuck', had been a big Irish hit for one of the biggest showbands. Pete Briquette, the bass player in the Rats, had come from the country (hence the name – peat briquette – look it up!). He hated the showbands and their shit nonsense. He suggested that it would be a laugh to invent our own ridiculous dance as a piss-take of the whole thing. I thought that was a brilliant idea and that night wrote a song that incorporated a series of the worst possible rodent-influenced puns with a completely undanceable dance in a classic 50s type rock 'n' roll "homage" that the showbands used to eviscerate every night. It became a hit!! It became our logo! What can you do? Do The Rat!

Do The Rat

He rodent into town
Fangs were getting him down
He whiskered around the juke joint
Where the cool cats hung around
Down at The Mouse Trap
Fangs were getting hot
Squealing with delight
Their legs began to hop

They're doin' The Rat
Keep your trap shut
Do The Rat
Be a cool cat
Do The Rat
Well hold on to your hat
'Cos that's where it's at
Wrap your tail around your partner
You're doing The Rat

You get down on the floor
Down on all fours
Sniffle with your nostrils
Scratch with your paws
Swish and swat that rodents tail
If you got little pink eyes
You just can't fail
Point your ear
Towards the stand
Listen to the music
Of that band
Your teeth are yellow
Your hair is gray
You'll be doin' The Rat
Until the break of day

You gotta make sewer
You're doin' it right
Scavenge on the dance floor

BOB GELDOF

All of the night
Don't get trapped in some corner
Or caught in a fight
You need all the strength
You got for doin' The Rat

Band Aid...

I got home about 6. I'd been trying to get 'Dave' moving all day. Motivate the record company. Work out some scam to get us on Top Of The Pops, after which things would make their own momentum. Pre-occupied with my depressive thoughts. I was on the sofa and the Missus beside me. She was about to put Baby 1 to bed, and I flipped channels to watch the national news on the BBC.

They showed something that put any stupid pathetic personal problems into a terrifying perspective and into sharp relief. A comfortable, warm home in Chelsea with a healthy baby and happy mother against the horrifying pornography of starving human beings. Children in emaciated agony. The uncomprehending pitiful eyes of mothers. The terrible impotence of the stick-like fathers. The awesome urgent dignity of these people against my stupid privileged bullshit. It was teatime in London, and we were watching the great African famine of 1984. Then. Now. At that exact precise moment. Something should be done...

Sometimes I wonder what would have happened if 'Dave' had been a hit? Would I even have been home to see the news? Would someone have called me the next day and said, "Did you see that thing on telly last night? Yea well I want to make a Xmas record and I was wondering if you'd be on it...?" And would I have been one of the ones who said, "Yes, of course"? Would I? God, I hope so...

BOB GELDOF / MIDGE URE

Do They Know It's Christmas?

It's Christmastime
and there's no need to be afraid
At Christmastime,
we let in light and we banish shade
And in our world of plenty,
We can spread a smile of joy
Throw your arms around the world
At Christmastime

But say a prayer
Pray for the other ones
At Christmastime it's hard,
But when you're having fun
There's a world outside your window
And it's a world of dread and fear
Where the only water flowing
Is the bitter sting of tears
And the Christmas bells that ring there
Are the clanging chimes of doom
Well tonight, thank God it's them instead of you

And there won't be snow in Africa this Christmastime
The greatest gift they'll get this year is life
Where nothing ever grows,
No rain nor rivers flow
Do they know it's Christmastime at all?

Here's to you, raise a glass for everyone
Here's to them, underneath that burning sun
Do they know it's Christmastime at all?

Feed the world
Let them know
It's Christmastime
Again

Doesn't Matter Now

The days are long
The nights are too
I'm sitting here
So where are you
I don't know who I'm talking to
It doesn't matter now

Every day seems like the other
You cling to one
And here comes another
I wonder who you're clinging to
It doesn't matter now

The daylight slowly fading makes me restless
The lonely twilight falling down
Sitting here makes me feeling desperate

And I'm getting old
The nights are blue
Thinking back
To when we were new
I guess I only borrowed you
It doesn't matter now

BOB GELDOF

Doin' It Right

O yeah, o yeah
She come on like a hurricane
You know she's something else again
Y'know she's doing it right

O yea o yea
Dancing at the Moonlight Ball
Shuffling through the new snowfall
And doin' it right

Every time I go to close my eyes
She's looming up into my sight
It gets so hard to be so blinkered
So blind
I can't close my eyes
When I'm going to sleep at night

O yea o yea
I was talking to the policeman
He said that he's our biggest fan
I said you're doin' it right

But o no o no
They're closing up the honky tonk
I said I think you're doing something wrong
They said we're doin' it right

Don't Believe What You Read

As soon as I wake up every day,
I look at the papers to see what they say,
I know most what I read will be a lot of lies,
But then you learn really fast to read between the lines,
Cos I know
What I read ain't true
I know
And I'm telling you
I know
If they say it's red, it's blue,
Don't believe what you read,
Do you believe what you read?
No, I don't believe what I read.

Never put it down in writing the old man said
I didn't know then but now I know what he meant,
And if you're wondering why your letters never get a reply,
It's just when you tell me that you love me
I need to see your eyes
Cos I know
What I read ain't true
I know
And I'm telling you
I know
If they say it's one, it's two
Don't believe what you read

And if you pick up a book and you're starting to read it,
I'll tell you what you'd better do,
You can read it till the end and even if you believe it,
That doesn't mean to say it's true

Don't believe what you read.

BOB GELDOF

Don't Talk To Me

You don't have to be afraid
You just have to make the leap of fate
I'm not thinking in quantum jumps no
I think in lines and
Speak in lumps
When you say those things, you seem so crude
Do you think you're clever, ah you're so rude

Please don't talk to me when I'm talking to you
Don't talk to me when I'm talking to you
Don't talk to me when I'm talking to you
Your mouth's wide open and it don't become you

No, there's no need to be ashamed
I'm left standing in the shade
But I say one thing you say another
I've got insurance, I'm well covered
You seem so real but you feel so fake
I got it made when I'm on the make

But don't talk to me when I'm................

I keep feelin' I've been framed
You stitch me up, now I'm tailor made
Time moves slow n you move quick
I stay static and I feel sick n
You toss and turn stay up all night n
Then you say those things and I don't know why

Don't talk to me................

MONDO BONGO, (U.S. RELEASE) 1981

Drag Me Down

Drag me down in colours pink and gold
(Like a ship that's going under
Bring me home in rain and thunder)
Bless the night before the day grows old
(In pink + gold)

It's just a moment of terror
A fraction of bliss
Your heart's in my mouth and
My soul's in your wrist
I love you I think
But is it always like this with you?

Tuck me up with stories I've been told
(Like a ship that's going under...
I'll be home in rain and thunder)
Then wake me up with days that come and go
(In pink and gold)

And when the record is over
The passion's been spent
The movie winds down and says "The End" in French
I'll tell all the lies
But do I have to pretend it's true?

I love you
And
I need you

Drive On Damo...

Then a country song to illustrate to the other bands that 'Anything they can do/We can do better'. It's just we chose not to. We wanted loud, fast, fuck off ... This was written for our first roadie. He had a van and was what today would be called a stoner. Slow, a quiet perma-smile, useless.

Drive On Damo

And you can – Drive on Damo
We gotta turn left but you always turn right
Drive on Damo
We might be there tomorrow but it's supposed to be tonight
Drive on Damo
He only opens his mouth to yawn
Driving on into the dawn

It's not that he's bored, he just chooses to ignore whatever's said to him,
Alive but asleep his hands rest on the wheel hip
He'll get you there but I don't think he cares
About the hours that lie ahead,
He's got a big bad load and a 100-mile road
And he's got to kill that black of dead

And you can – Drive on Damo
We gotta turn left but you always turn right
Drive on Damo
We might be there tomorrow but it's supposed to be tonight
Drive on Damo
He only opens his mouth to yawn
Driving on into the dawn

So, miles down outta cold Town and then he started slowing down,
We had checked all the gears in the front and the rear
And couldn't find anything wrong
Until somebody noticed the petrol gauge was hovering around the red

Drive-on just smiled and said it don't matter
Anyhow there's a station 'bout 8 miles ahead

BOB GELDOF

The Elephant's Graveyard

America, too – that older ex-colony still cannot reconcile within itself today. How or why the African-American population puts up with the manifest and glaring injustice visited upon its population is simply beyond me. How the white population allows it disgusts me. They are lucky the black population maintains its restraint and dignity through every insult. Is it an inherited African sense of fatalism that I am familiar with or was it beaten into people via the slavery of an earlier America? Certainly, it's there in the music I love. The classic blues trope: "Woke up this morning..." and things are still bad or getting worse. The beautiful blues "Woke up this morning ... it's shit."

There had been riots in Miami while we were there. Bad riots. When they ended three days later, 18 people were dead and 800 injured. Needless to say, they were all black people. Black lives have *always* seemed to matter less. It began when four cops killed a black insurance agent and were acquitted. Course they were.

In my head, Miami was where older, wealthier Americans went to die in relative comfort. Warmth, fellow aged for company, golf, beauty shops for the blue-rinsed pensioners and beach boy gigolos for those ol' gals and geezers still up for it.

An elephant's graveyard alongside Disneyland and the town Disney were building specifically for those 'seniors' who could afford the cartoon calm of an unstated but obviously made-for-whites-only, gated, secure, end-of-life Potemkin village. Imagine then the shock when what lay beyond the facade came crashing through the gates – if only figuratively through the television screen, the newspaper photographs and the distant view and stench of smoke from burning buildings.

I do not say that in either spite or glee, but in fear that all of America then as now, can be viewed through the same lens. That's how I experience America. How afraid everyone is. How uncomfortable they are with their nation. How it explains the sentimental, teary-eyed mawkishness over flags and anthems and the noisome insistence of exceptionalism and the other shibboleths of silly 'greatness'. Like a tiresome carapace disguising deep paranoia and insecurity and the existential tensions they give rise to. Everyone secretly seems to suspect that all of America might be a systemic lie, the thinnest veneer, a thin ice of a wildly unsustainable asymmetric society. Amongst many other things, and most importantly, a proportion of America's people will not be overtly humiliated, dispossessed, imprisoned, put down or put upon, beaten down or beaten up without America at some point breaking.

It is not enough to simply stop saying a derogatory noun. Stopping saying 'nigger' means nothing when the word finds its own reality in housing, jobs, schooling, justice, prisoner figures and on and on. The word is shocking because of its implication, but its implication made flesh is the true sickening outrage. Language is magical. Words have power. People are insulted by that word. It hurts. It wounds. Others feel sick when they hear people use it. They are right. But what exactly shocks them? Is it that behind that word lies a whole system of injustice and exclusion and oppression made tangible in the real world of many, many black Americans? That one person can be considered somehow less, of less value by virtue of something as facile as the colour of one's skin? Isn't that really it? Isn't that so intellectually preposterous? So banal. And yes I know 'profanity is indicative of the lazy mind' but isn't it so fucking stupid?

'Justice isn't blind
It just looks the other way.
Not from want of trying
I have nothing left to say.'

And I haven't.

BOB GELDOF

The Elephant's Graveyard

Did you slip the noose when the beast broke loose
The elephant's graveyard ain't the place to be.
And white turns black, dies of heart attack
The elephant's graveyard needs the change of scene.
You got the money, but who needs the tension
And fear's no cheaper on the old age pension
There's just one thing that I forgot to mention
What've you got to lose when you know

You're guilty till proven guilty
Isn't that the law
Guilty till proven guilty
That's what we saw.

Do the blue rinse shuffle with the beach boy muscle
The elephant's graveyard ain't the place to be.
Waiting all your life for this golf cart life
The elephant's graveyard needs the change of scene.
You see the judge and then you check the jury
She does her hair and calls the lawyer cutie
It's Disneyland under martial law
Switch on the TV tell me what you saw

You're guilty till proven guilty
Isn't that the law
Guilty till proven guilty
That's what we saw.

Justice isn't blind
It just looks the other way.
Not from want of trying
I have nothing left to say.

The sky burns bright, 24 hour night
The elephant's graveyard ain't the place to be.
And you don't pay death duties when you're on death duty
The elephant's graveyard needs the change of scene.
You came here looking for the peace and quiet
The healthy air and the healthy diet
The sea's so calm but the street's a riot
Taken years off your life when you've no years left to give
You're guilty till proven guilty

Shame.

BOB GELDOF
The End Of The World

Though it strikes you as seeming a little absurd
I'm here to announce the end of the world
It'll happen sometime between now and high noon
It doesn't give you much time as it's happening real soon
It'll start with a whimper it'll end with a bang
It'll leave a big hole where we could have sang

This is the end
The end of the world
For five thousand years
You must surely have heard
Nostradamus and Jesus and Buddha and me
We said it was coming
Now just wait and see

So everyone outside look up at the sky
It's the last time you'll see it so wave it goodbye
You took it for granted you thought it was free
Say goodbye to the leaves the trees and the sea
There's nothing more useless than a car that won't start
But it's even more useless at the end of the world.

Europe Looked Ugly

It's odd being old. The histories we lived in seem to bear little relation to the lives of our children, save that their repercussions and reverberations shape their world as much as the reality did ours.

It is weird to speak like a bunch of oul' fellas (which we are) of living under the nuclear threat as a tangible prepared for thing that was bound to happen any day soon. That this was a real, felt fear in our everyday lives. But here's the thing... it still is. Indeed, it's worse. Any fucking headbanger out there could let one of these things off. And yet, no one seems that bothered anymore. Or they have an 'Oh well, not much we can do about it now' attitude. Which may be true, but still... come on... Maybe a *que sera sera* shrug is healthier than our duplicitous diving under our school desk fallout drills when the church bells ring fatuities.

Or the Iron Curtain. Talking about Communists or the Soviet bloc seems almost as anachronistic and irrelevant as discussing the impact of the Hanoverian Palatinate (whatever that was). But it was real and it was awful. Half a continent unfree to speak or think or behave without either the harshest imprisonment or application, and condescending approved permissions for which one should be grateful. The grinding overwhelming power of brute dictatorship, desperate for a legitimacy spuriously allowed for under the aegis of a romantic but wrong-headed ideology. 'Great idea. Wrong species' as the philosopher and biologist E.O. Wilson accurately put it.

We travelled and played a lot through those smothered peoples and their crazy, crazed and perverse regimes. Romania I think was the worst, but they were all sad, muted places. Physically beautiful countries but dilapidated, hopeless towns and cities, economies and peoples. Hopeless in the literal sense of the word. Short of killing everyone (though they tried that too), how did they ever imagine that you could stifle people and their imagination and aspirations forever? Madness. Autocracy will always fail because it can never give people that which they ultimately require, which is freedom.

But trawling through the drab winters on the never-ending ribbons of roads, 'our' side often seemed as worn-out and exhausted by the argument as the other. There was a sort of James Bond-type thrill, waiting and crossing through from one patch onto the other. Famously, Checkpoint Charlie was the most acute. The place where the 20th century achieved its seedy, visible and deadly chess game apogee. Here all the murderous wars met in a mutually agreed stalemate.

And the awfulness of that Wall, with its graffiti sprayed one side and blood stained other, reared up left and right and on forever in its concrete metaphor of the truth.

We queued overnight at yet another border crossing to have our carnets, visas and passports intensely and suspiciously scrutinised by glowering, chillingly unfriendly, staring, multi-armoured guards, soldiers or plain-clothes secret service geezers. As though us – smelly, tired, grumpy, slept-in clothes, rumpled dope-smelling bus, unemptied chemical toilet, attitudinally suspect musical gangsters – were about to be personally responsible for bringing the whole sham down around their naked fears.

Cos as it turned out, that's what did happen and those dull emperors, despite their block-cut ill-fitting suits, really did have no clothes on all that time. We liked to think that we were partially responsible for that. Actually, I have no doubt that rock 'n' roll was part of it. In many respects, rock 'n' roll is just the manic noise that capitalism would make if it bought itself a guitar.

It's that drab and tired 'our side' I wrote about in 'Europe Looked Ugly'. Not a successful track – a B-side I think, but retrospectively it takes me accurately back to then. And then the miracle that none of my kids could understand or care about really. The real Great Escape from that continental Colditz, when an entire people scrabbled at the breeze blocks and cement of history till their nails were bloodied, until, like a great dam bursting, they flooded into the beginning of the 21st century.

Europe Looked Ugly

Europe looked ugly
The very last time that I saw her
Cold and so empty
She sucks on her gums and looks tired
She picks up her skirts
Still coy but no longer worth knowing
She grins toothlessly
I could see the light die in her eyes

I'm taking my time
I won't hurry
I'll sit and I'll watch
The last train won't leave for a while
And the buildings themselves seem to sag
From the effort of standing
While the trees and the people are bent
From the effort of dying

So I watched from the window
As she opened her legs wide before me
And the track through the bile leave trails
Like a steel slug on slime
Well me I keep thinking 'bout the iron
That surrounds and protects her
Cos a chastity belt for a whore seems
Almost sublime

What do we do now?
With you and your stories
We feel sorry for you

I don't like my body,
The things that it needs just disgust me
I don't like my mind
The things that I think aren't quite sane
But I can still function as normal
So long as my mouth moves
I think it's the culture
I'm lucky they can't see my brain

What do we do now?

Europe looked ugly the very last time that I saw her

BOB GELDOF

Fall Down

Put your head between your knees and breathe real deep
Let it in
Let it out
Until it's over.

I might scribble, I might scrawl
I might claw at the wall
I might storm and rage and thunder
Oh Christ but then later
In the incinerator
Something inside seems to fall asunder.

I need to scream every now and again
Try to understand it's only me
Not only cripples have a need for crutches
And if they
Ever take
You away
From me

I'd fall down
Fall down and lie still
Moving in for the kill
Fall down
Putting several boots in
Lie helpless
God help us
Our heads up
We'd scream

Put your head between your knees and breathe real deep
Let it in
Let it out
Until it's over.

Fanzine Hero

Sissy was a bright young thing
She know all the latest hit songs
She flashed her eyes
Wriggled her thighs
Every time her favourite singer come on
Yes she loved the way he moved his hips
She copied it every time
She loses her senses and she visibly melts
When he flashed her up one of his smiles

Sissy saved up all of her money
Pumped it down the record store drain
She bought all the latest hit records
She nearly drove her parents insane

He was her fanzine hero
He couldn't do anything wrong
He wasn't of this earth at all
But she knew exactly where he comes from
Yeah she knew his favourite colour
And she knew his favourite car
And she knew his favourite country
And knew his songs off by heart

Well Sissy girl you're so young
Don't throw your love away on him
He's only vaguely aware that you're out there
When he checks his royalty returns

He was her fanzine hero...

Fanzine heroes are all much the same
Super-hip dudes with a fancy name
Is it Sissy or the hero, tell me who's to blame
At the whole money spinning, manipulation game
And she gave him all her money
Pumped it down the record store drain
She bought all his single hit records
She nearly drove her parents insane

BOB GELDOF

He was her fanzine hero...

O Sissy girl you're so young
Don't throw your love away on him
He's only vaguely aware that you're out there
When he checks his royalty returns

The Fields Of Spring

Lay me down by some fields and streams
And I'll watch the sky roll over me
And I'll roll
Off to bed
Before the night comes on

Golly gee, she's in love with me
And I said yippee
And she said "let's see"
So we stroll
Off our heads
Before the night was done
But I need it
Can't you see it
Tugging at this vacant heart tonight
I'm on empty
Give me plenty
Through my veins and skin
I'm gonna let it in
The world is looking
Much too thin
For us tonight

And so let my soul
Out to play again
And so let my soul
Say it's ok again

Lay me down in the fields of spring
And like the flowers
I'll re-begin
Make me whole
With unimagined lives
That nourish me
Do you feel it
Can you see it
Like a double Red Bull
Rushing through my veins alright

BOB GELDOF

I'm going out there
And no I'm not scared
Yeah relish the wine
And love the light
I'm gonna make this ol' world
Dance around our moon tonight

And so let my soul out to play again
And so let my soul say it's ok again
Lay me down in the fields of spring
And we'll watch the clouds roll over me
Let 'em roll

For Those Who Travel Lonely ...

I'd 'sort of' written what I thought were 'songs' long before the Rats. I say 'sort of' because although they were songs, they were completely derivative. However, they remain accurate of what was happening to me at the time and therefore serve a purpose of being diary notes to the self. This one was written while I hitchhiked up and down England looking for any work I could get. I slept wherever I ended up at nightfall. Under trees, in fields, abandoned cars, warm heating outlets of buildings, bus shelters, church crypts, the occasional kindness of a room and sometimes a legitimate B 'n' B. It wasn't romantic and I hated it.

I got lucky in the summer of '72. I was working on the building of the M23 motorway. One of the drivers of the big Terex T24 digging machines had got drunk once too often and had been fired. The gangerman on the crew told the foreman that 'Dublin here' (i.e. Me) could drive. I couldn't, but Don showed me how and I began to earn serious money with the wildest bunch of beyond-the-reach outlaws I'd ever met hitherto. If I could save enough, I could get to the next place, wherever that was and the next job, whatever that may be. The thing was to keep moving. There had to be something out there for me, you just had to go looking for it. Maybe you'd get lucky and find it ...

BOB GELDOF

For Those Who Travel Lonely ...

When evenings twilight glimmer
Starts to fading
And dusk has told you
That it's time to leave
Dusty dusty traveller
The night-time is no friend
Better find a roof and
Catch up on lost sleep

And for those who travel
Lonely on the road
Here's a few good
Honest home truths
Need be told
Carry a light pack
Full of everything
That you might lack
And keep your head and heart
Free and easy
And take it easy

When Winters bitter chill
Begins to tighten
And biting winds freeze
Words inside your mouth
Traveller turn your head
Another road and someplace else
Are calling to your feet
Turning South

And for those who travel
Lonely on the road
Here's a few good
Honest home truths
Need be told
Carry a light pack
Full of everything
That you might lack
And keep your head and heart
Free and easy
And take it easy

...Free and easy
And that ain't easy

Friends For Life

I can be your friend
A friend like me you need
I can be your lunch
When you need to feed
I can be your boss
Baby you been fired
I can be your sleep
When you're feeling tired
Yes I could be a friend for life
Baby if you want me to

Just let me take you on that
Boat ride, plane ride, somehow
Get me out of here
Let me be the one to say this once
Let me make it clear
You could be my friend for life
Baby if you wanted to

I could be the back
For you to lean upon
I could be your leg
For you to jump down on
I could be your arms
Administering the pill
See this broken back
It's broken at your will

I could be your shoes
Take me walking, slip me on
See this little face
It's a seat to sit upon
I could be your boss
And baby you've been fired
I could be your plug
Connect me when you're wired

BOB GELDOF

Get A Grip...

Get a grip baby
Get a grip on yourself
You're on some kinda trip
And it can't be good for your health

She's doing
Heroin, ketamine
Crack cocaine,
Amphetamines
She's pilled up
It builds up
The hole that's never
Filled up
It's hard core
Drug store
Looking for the next score
Give it up
Can't give it up
It's more, more, more more...

She gonna upload her tit shots
Everybody says she's hot
A meme queen
Teen dream
Ten thousand billion likes are keen
She's meta-data
5 Star rated
A brand new cyber star created
Just another little suckered girl
Gives it up for Zuckerberg
Yea...

Go

My killer came in crinolines
Pounding at the door
And of course she wanted shelter
But of course I knew the score
And of course I needed love
And of course she needed more
As she stood like frozen Liberty
Some statue on my porch

Well whaddya know
When it's time to go
You gotta go

The gutters ran with blood that night
And the sluices slashed like blades
And the storm that seemed to brew there
Came down in cloth-like veils
And she looked like she was ruined
As she stepped up to that plate
But I eased her every step back down
And that was my mistake

But whaddya know
When it's time to go
You gotta go

BOB GELDOF

Go Man Go!

I read a lot. On an average day I'll have two or three books on the go with a slab of poetry on the side. I keep most of the books. Can't throw 'em out. And when I see them all lined up in a vague order of subject matter or whatever, I feel a sort of comfort. Weird, I know. When my eye falls upon some book I read long ago and I no longer remember its precise contents, some atavistic 'book memory' stirs in the deep down somewhere and provokes a vague inchoate sense of excitement, reminding me that I read this once and I thought it was great. And then I make a resolution to pull it out and read it once more, but I never do. It just remains a feeling on a shelf.

All of this started at 3 or 4. I went to the kindergarten at my sister's convent school. The nuns taught us our letters and numbers. Letters were sandpaper cut-outs stuck to a light blue piece of thin cardboard. We had to close our eyes and trace the contours of whichever letter we were learning that day, whilst lengthily vocalising the phonetic sound of the particular symbol. 'Buuuuh' or 'Rrrruh' for 'B' or 'R', etc. You *felt* the sound through your finger on the sandpaper. Eyes tightly shut, the letter etched itself as a physical thing onto the frontal cortex. Or maybe even deeper. These symbols had texture and depth and weight ... and they still do. People sometimes say that words are weighted. They are for me. They are physical things. Speaking is like being a juggler tossing word-objects into the air and catching them in precise order of coherence, complexity and structure in order to express feeling, sense and thought. Language is magical.

There was no telly at home even in my teen years. There was the radio – speech, and there were comics, newspaper and books from school. I could read at 6. That was the entertainment. Still is. Just give me the missus, my books, my guitar, some wine and somewhere to walk and I'm done.

Newspapers have always been fodder for songs. Mind you, you take your cues, the 'song-hit', from anywhere you can grab it. Anything might spark you off, but usually it's the individual writer's natural inclinations that will respond to different stimuli. John Lennon from the poster on his wall or the morning paper, or Dylan's newspaper or book. They're geniuses though, but still it's the same logic for even the plodders in the 'Tower Of Song'.

We were going round the world and the world seemed to be going mad. 'Mondo Bongo'. We'd just left Japan where they had poisoned Tokyo Bay with a chemical discharge of mercury. Stinking dead fish floated on slurping tides and clogged the waterways. Where people walked around with flu-masks on their faces and Walkman (the latest in whizz-bang technology) headphones clamped on their heads. Through the fog of jet-lag and the sensory overload of constant difference, it all seemed an oddly dystopian world of environmental terror blended with authoritarian indifference and public passivity or purposeful ignorance.

And I was just tired. Man, I just wanted to be at home. ('Go Man Go!')

BOB GELDOF

Go Man Go!

These are danger days
What sort of day is this?
These are troubled times
D'ya know what time it is?
There it goes again
Another gear being slipped
I must be near the sea
A single cod n' chips
A cup a tea for 3
An' 6 including V.A.T.
Around the rugged rocks
A round trip there and back
The helter-skelter's free
(Don't tell mad Charlie that)
I'd send a bloody card
But he'd want a bloody snap.

I'd stay at home today
But the world said
Go man go
Everybody said
Go man go
The postman said
Go man go
Oy, oy vey

I feel so down, so low, too tired to think
I feel so low, oh no, well what do you think?
My feet slow down, ah so well, I can't lift my head
A fevered brow, ho no, think I'll stay here in bed
Thunder over Tokyo
Pressure on my eyes
Hi-fi on their heads
While they tidy their tides
Dear Auntie Fifi
You should see this place
They'd grow a cushion on your back,
An' a flu mask on your face

BOB GELDOF

I'd stay at home today
But the world said
Go man go
In Japanese they said
Hayacho cho wazza woko
I heard someone say
Go man go
And we went
Oy vey.

BOB GELDOF

Good Boys In The Wrong

Waiting for the phone to ring
Willie starts to iron things
Annie changed the sheets today
Now rockin time is here to stay
We are good boys in the wrong
(Don't say that, you know you shouldn't say that)
Just wind me up and sing along
Cos rockin time has almost gone

I'm gonna talk about time
Moving slow
And I move slowly with it
I don't know
If I can jump and swing it
I'll take a chance
And wing it
Start me up
And help me get away

Davey watch his tv screen
Yea jump and shout you groovy thing
If everybody thought this way
Then rockin time would always stay
But now we're talking 'bout
Time moving slow
And I move slowly with it
If I can jump and swing it
I'll take a chance and wing it
Start me up
And help me get away

The Great Song Of Indifference

I don't mind if you go
I don't mind if you take it slow
I don't mind if you say yes or no
I don't mind at all

I don't care if you live or die
Couldn't care less if you laugh or cry
I don't mind if you crash or fly
I don't mind at all

I don't mind if you come or go
I don't mind if you say no
Couldn't care less baby let it flow
'Cause I don't care at all

Na, na, na...

I don't care if you sink or swim
Lock me out or let me in
Where I'm going or where I've been
I don't mind at all

I don't mind if the government falls
Implements more futile laws
I don't care if the nation stalls
And I don't care at all

I don't care if they tear down trees
I don't feel the hotter breeze
Sink in dust in dying seas
And I don't care at all

Na, na, na...

I don't mind if culture crumbles
I don't mind if religion stumbles
I can't hear the speakers mumble
And I don't care at all

BOB GELDOF

I don't care if the third world fries
It's hotter there I'm not surprised
Baby I can watch whole nations die
And I don't care at all

I don't mind, I don't mind, I don't mind
I don't mind, I don't mind,
I don't mind, I don't mind at all

Na, na, na...

I don't mind about people's fears
Authority no longer hears
Send a social engineer
'Cos I don't mind at all

The Happy Club

Every morning
'Bout the break of day
Every evening
She comes up and she says
Na, Na, Na

She gets up
Then she goes outside
She don't know what she does
But it feels all right
She says I
I'm a sunny girl
Yeah I'm feeling good
And it's a shiny world
Well here she comes

She feels good
She feels great today
When I asked she said
"Hey, it's the Happy Club way"
I don't know
I don't know what to do
But I know if I could
Then I would do too

I feel great
I feel fine today
I joined the Happy Club
And the Happy Club says
I feel good
I feel great today
Now I know what to say
Na, Na, Na

BOB GELDOF

Hard Times

I had known London. At first living 'on the street' – sometimes literally. Finding a building's exhaust or tube vent or grill and grabbing a quick kip in the blowing bad-for-you warm air. But usually those sites were already occupied and violently guarded by older hands holding damaged lives of alcoholic or junked-out indifference. Or just sadder folk who had lost their way or never had a way in the first place.

Better nights were spent in the crypt of the beautiful Baroque church opposite High Holborn tube station. A few years on from this point, the Rats would have their office right beside that church. All lives turn on a coin. Or in my case, turn on a tune.

I think it was 50p to get a thin sponge mattress to lie on and a space on the crypt floor amongst the other ruins of the night. I think there was tea and some bread or something in the early morning before we all had to clear out and make our way through the next day.

I was afraid. I had become those people I had worked amongst in Dublin a few years before. It wasn't romantic or fun being one of the lost and broke. The future could not be one of nothing.

I worked my way up to a squat. At last there was a base. Tufnell Park NW10 was an uninspiring HQ for Project Bob to start but I could begin to assemble myself at least. I had a kind girlfriend, I had a guitar, I had the cinema queues and the tube stations and with the odd dope deal for a bit of the ol' extra-curricular wedge maybe, just maybe, ... y'know?

But the London I met with the Rats was from another planet entirely. As Shelley said of this great city, 'In its depths what treasures! You will see ..." We did.

Punk, as the man in the movie said, "Blew the bloody doors open". We weren't punks but we shared the attitude. The effect of the band in Ireland the previous year had mirrored the reaction of the UK to this newer energy. We dived straight in.

Hard Times

And these are hard times
They're getting better,

I straighten out n' checkin'
Out that drag
You're touch an' go
But I'm touching you
Spare a dime, or at least a thousand P...
It's tasting sweet
The love you like to eat
On yer bike
You got them goods
You stash that cash
And then you pedal away
The only act of revolution left
In this collective world
Is thinking for yourself

So look good, talk good
And don't turn away
You look all right
And I feel okay
If things are like this
Then maybe we'll stay
Turn away
Don't turn away

All dressed in blue
Oh she stops the street
The day pulls up
And all the bulls see red
Like that Pope
I'll kiss the ground below
Tasting sweet
The love you like to eat
Brush a tooth and wipe the night away
It's tasting sour
Of dreams and fright

BOB GELDOF

But I swear, I swear right now
In that bitter sleep
I think that I found peace

Oh I've been lying
In the long grass too long
Pushing back the psychic wheeds
Hit that switch
And knock the daylights out
Tasting sweet
The love you like to eat
Oh walk away
Walking through that door
It's open wide, but all the options close
Let me say, oh let me say right here
I'll dig my ditch
And keep my head down through these
Hard times

Harvest Moon

You got the love
And baby I got the heart
That needs it
Fill me up
Take me to the brim
I woke today
And after three years baby
I looked in the mirror
And saw my face again

Nobody speaks
Because nobody knows
Who they're talking to
The night wears on
And then its 3a.m.
So many nights
Waiting for that first light
Until I realised
I could go home again

Underneath that harvest moon
Baby me and you
And just like that old harvest moon
We'll make the world anew

You got the love
And baby I got the heart
That needs it
Fill me up
Until I overspill
You took my life
And baby who'd have believed it
I'm stepping out
And dressed to kill again

Underneath that harvest moon
Baby you and me
And just like that old harvest moon
We'll make the world anew.

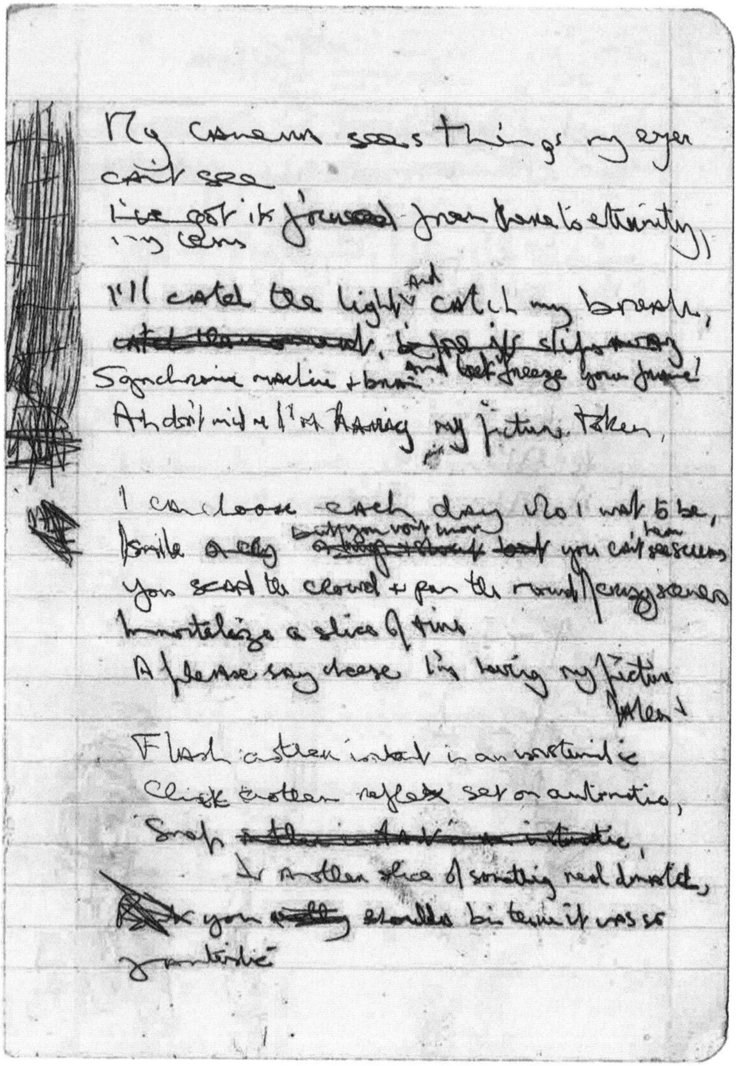

My camera sees things my eyes
can't see
~~I've~~ got its focused from here to eternity
my lens

I'll catch the light and catch my breath,
~~catch the moment, before it slips away~~
Synchronise machine + brain and let freeze your frame!
Ah don't mind me I'm having my picture taken,

I can choose each day who I want to be,
I smile ~~a lot~~ ~~...~~ you can't see seen
You scan the crowd + pan the round / crazy scenes
Immortalise a slice of time
A please say cheese I'm having my picture
taken!

Flash another instant in an instamatic
Click another reflex set on automatic,
Snap, ~~...~~,
It another slice of something real dramatic,
~~...~~ you ~~...~~ shouldn't be there it was so
fantastic

 'HAVING MY PICTURE TAKEN' EARLY DRAFT OF LYRICS

Having My Picture Taken

My camera,
Sees things my eyes can't see.
I have it focused,
From here to eternity.
Catch the moment, catch the light, catch your breath
Let me freeze your frame.
We'll synchronize machine and brain,
But don't mind me...
I'm having my picture taken.

I can choose
Each day who I want to be.
You can choose
Each day who you want to see,
We'll scan the crowd and pan the mounds
Of all those
Distant scenes,
Immortalize a slice of time,
Hey don't mind me...
I'm having my picture taken.

Flash: another instant in an instamatic,
Click: another reflex set on automatic,
Snap: another moment of the life dramatic,
You really should have been there
It was so fantastic

BOB GELDOF

He Watches It All

He bought and sold a video
Made a fortune in between
A thousand well-known faces
Passed across that stupid screen
He turned them down
He never thought they had much to say
He watched those faces come and go
Up close
He saw the strain
And he watches it all
Yes he watches it all

Someone broke into his house last night
It's strange they didn't take a thing
Someone broke into his house last night
But still it feels like they took everything
Home is where the head is
Home is where the demons all come out to play
Home is where you hide yourself at night
And home is where you feel safe
And still he watches it all
He watches it all
And it's small
It all seems small

Did you read it in the Sunday paper?
The headline called him the 'Sailors Deacon'
He fell in love with the lighthouse keeper
Spends his time bringing home the beacon
Huh
He bought and sold a video
Made a fortune in between

Her Turn Tonight

Stop all your crying
Don't let them see
The pain in your eyes
Don't let it show
Don't let her know
That it affects you
And when she says
She's leaving today
One thing is certain
She's going to pay
Revenge is too sweet
When she says to me
It's her turn tonight

She made all your life
A ruin and misery
She counted up the days
'Til she turned to me
And she swore it'll be
Me tonight

Inside you were dead
When you heard it said
That she really hates you
But the part that's alive
Said only survive
Don't let hate betray you
The dish best served cold
Is still there on hold
The time will be right
To unsheathe the knife
That green in her eyes
Will tell you it's time
For her turn tonight

BOB GELDOF

Here's A Postcard...

Here she comes
Walking down the street
Hi-heeled shoes and her mini-skirt
And her heat
It's a summers day in London
All the kids are out on the street
It's too hot, it's too hot
You get excited
Gotta cool down honey
You got that London beat
We say Yeah!

Meanwhile back up Shady Alley
Cats and dogs can barely breathe
The sky is golden
That air is molten
The tar is bubbling up beneath your feet
You wanna walk?
Well stay cool
You wanna walk?
Gotta stay cool
Ice-cream music in the park
Ice-cream melting in the park
You buy your ice-cream
And you eat your ice-cream
And the day moves on
Like in a passing dream

You walk on down
You hit the bar
Inside the bar the guys are talking to the girls
The girls have nothing on and you can see the world
You say
"O my God amen
On days like this it's good to be a man"
And the summer keeps on coming
And the heat keeps swirling 'round
And suddenly the sun in its floating sky
Drops just as quick to cooling night

You wanna hear the heat?
Yea
Are you sure you really wanna feel the heat?
Yea
You wanna know what it sounds like?
Yes
Are you really sure you wanna know what it feels like?
Yea
Well it sorta goes something like this...

Here's a postcard
Of a Summers day

BOB GELDOF

Here's To You

Here's to you and all our friends
May God protect us
Until the very end
All the places that we go
And everybody that we know
And every single living thing
The earth, the sky, the wind, the sea
O I'm in love with you tonight
Yea I'm in love with Life tonight
And y'know I think that's right

So, let it rain, let it rain

Hotel 75

Down at Hotel 75
(Shout it out Bob)
There's a note saying
"Hi we're glad you arrived"
(Shout it out Bob)
And without any further
Reason or rhyme
They check you
Out of Room 3
In to Room 49
There's a part of me thinks that I've been lying
But you know it's true

Hotel 75 is stuck
Somewhere down the 60's gut
They keep the inmates well supplied
With all they need to stay alive
They even give them things to drive them all
Up their papered walls

Hotel 75
They're glad you came
Hotel 75
Why can't you stay
And give it one more day
Just one more day

Someone spoke
But they talked too loud
And pretty soon they'd got a crowd
And as they declaimed from the mezzanine
Someone rang a magazine
Do a story on the kings and queens and brides
Of times gone by
The woman at the door
Is looking for a fuse
To help recharge her failing muse
It left her stranded and subdued

BOB GELDOF

I said "excuse me if I seem amused
I too have the hotel blues"
And she said "no, you're quite mistaken
I've been had and I've been taken"
I said "that's no more than me"
And she said "yes, possibly
But you should try and really see
The things I've done
The things I've been
Pardon me but have you seen
The list here with the hotel rooms
Where no one gets the hotel blues
No one fights
Friend or foe
When you're done
You don't know
It's another world here
Don't you know?"

The House At The Top Of The World

I got off the 45A somewhere around the new estates which were advertised as being in Killiney but were really in just a field. And I was going to the house at the top of the world.

Brian Carroll lived around here somewhere. And after school I'd sometimes go back to his place and sing with his brother Dermot. He knew all the Motown songs. Sometimes I think about him and I heard that he's a civil servant in Cork which is funny for a guy who used to sing Motown songs.

Soon I'd come to the Leopardstown dual carriageway. It was the first motorway in Ireland and it was a 100 yards long. I liked the name. I don't remember a town being there and I certainly saw no leopards. But I had to cross it anyway to get to the house at the top of the world.

Everyone thought the dual carriageway was great and modern and every Saturday the bowsies, yahoos, guttersnipes and corner boys would empty out of the pubs and scream like wild Saturday night leopards drunk and fast and delirious for that blessed 100 yards. People were always getting killed.

Well I ducked and weaved and it was fun and I made it over and up the small road, past the Silver Tassie, along the river bank past the Proddie church and off left up the lane to the house at the top of the world where you lived.

Your mother in her sensible shoes and your father in his tea-cosy woolly hat, bright eyes and roomful of old hoarded yellowing newspapers and 1920's photos of the Burren and you busy in the kitchen half-glad to see me, half nervous with your parents around.

BOB GELDOF

You'd take me for a walk around the field and down the lane and when the evening fell your father would light the peat fire and show me pictures of the West taken in the 20's and then he'd go to bed. And the night was full of you and the evening and the peat fire in the house on the top of the world.

And then it was time to go and risk death again in the dark of the Leopardstown dual carriageway.
And on the way back
I felt I could just jump the whole bloody thing.

House On Fire

I heard Tarzan outside playing on the Jungle Blues
I know cos I saw him shimmer in a Kenyan pool
Coming on in the vines with his leopard-skin loincloth cool
Bony Watusi fingers
Beating on the bark of a tree
Now Tarzan and me, well, obviously we're like that
Me and Tarzan, yeah, we get on like a house on fire

Look at cool Louise she's the one with the knick-knack eyes
She's only 17 but she knows how to make boys fight
Yeah she'll slit you with her eyes an' she'll slash you
with her cut-back smile
Ah she's as cruel as a pig but we love her like a house on fire
Louise and me now obviously we're like that
Me and the devil yeah we get on like a house on fire

I saw a raw white angel executing loop-de-loops in the sky
Drawing lazy spirals with his slipstream smoke as he silently
    passed us by
But his halo got too heavy so he hung it down around his waist
Doing halo hula-hoops, executing loop-de-loops takes a lot of
skill and bad taste
Now the angel and me, well, obviously we're like that
Yes me and the devil well we get on like a house on fire

BOB GELDOF

How Do You Do?

I'm tired of listening to you
I'm tired of hearing 'bout the things
I should or shouldn't do
All about the deals I blew
How do you do?

I shook a thousand hands
I met a man with master plans
And sweaty palms
Do you wanna be a rich man?
How do you do?

But then it's all right
The band played good
And it was Saturday night night
It was all right
And that's what matters
That really matters, sometimes that matters
The crowd went wild when they played The Slide

And then they sat me in a chair
Take this pen and put your name right there
This ensures that we take care of you

I don't know you
Who are you?
What do you do?
How do you do?

How I Roll

It's hard times
Trying to make a living
You wake up every morning
In the unforgiving
Out there
Somewhere in the city
There's people living lives
Without mercy or pity
It's how they roll

I feel good
Yeah I'm feeling fine
I feel better than I have for the longest time
I think these pills
Have been good for me
I think they banished
All my blues into infinity
That's how I roll

Sometimes I wake up at night
I don't know what it is
But I must have got a fright
I thought I heard a scratching
Underneath the floor
Does the devil come to get you
At a quarter to four?
It's how I roll

Too late
She cried out loud
Her voice emerging
From her inner shroud
Too much I thought
I heard her choke
It's all she says
After last year's stroke

BOB GELDOF

She has a hard time
Living in this city
She wakes up every morning
In the unforgiving
And out there
Somewhere in the city
There's people living lives
Without mercy or pity
It's how it rolls

Dear God, it's how they roll

'HUGE BIRDLESS SILENCE', EARLY DRAFT OF LYRICS

BOB GELDOF

Huge Birdless Silence

O you travelling ladies
I do not believe you
I am what I am
And I am not deceived

On a slow boat we drift
In horse latitude waters
Becalmed on the swells
Of the internal seas
And towing behind us
A huge birdless silence
The air is a hammer
The waters don't breathe

On a day like tomorrow
When all things are sacred
I'll lie like a drunk
'Gainst some sun-roasted wall
And the air will not move
And all time lies suspended
Between now and forever
Until darkness falls

Hurt Hurts

I don't want to listen
But I think I see you screaming
And it hurts.

Instant Solzhenitsyn
I get salt mines when I hear your voice
It hurts.

Kiss the hurt off her Kung Fu tongue
I turn off when she turns on
That's why I'll say
Hurts hurts.

Who an' what an' where an' when an' why an' how an'
Which you bitch
It hurts.

The false teeth shake an' rattle
When the slack mouth tittle tattles
And it hurts.

Kiss the hurt on her Kung Fu tongue
I come off when she comes on
That's why we say
Hurt hurts.

My ears are bleeding
My stomach's so sore

I slice the hurt off her Kung Fu tongue
We come off when they come on
That's why we say
Hurt hurts.

Hard hide
Tough inside
She cut you with stiletto style
Boy, it hurts.

BOB GELDOF

I lick the wound, she tears the eyes
You scratch her back and she'll claw mine
That hurts.

My eyes water
My mouth's so dry

Kiss the hurt off her Kung Fu tongue
I turn off when you turn on
Then I might say
Hoit hoits
Hurt hurts.

I Can Make It If You Can

Somewhere a screen door slammed
Somewhere, someplace, somebody's killing a man
Down the road I'm told five people died
And I wonder are you making love to anyone tonight?

Cos you and I, we're still sitting here
Our eyes are dry but we're bored to tears
She said let's talk about the future, let's forget about the past
But did I forget to tell you that the future never lasts

And can I hold on that long
Is it worth the same old stringalong
There's been a few rights but there's plenty wrongs
I can make it if you can.

Don't trust anything, especially love
Be careful of the broken bottles on the wall above.
They burn your brain and they'll tear at your mind
I know I won't be making love to anyone tonight.

Cos she and I we're still sitting here
Our eyes are dry but we're bored to tears.
Don't talk about the future, please don't talk about the past
Let's forget about the present, it makes me want to laugh.

'I CRY TOO' EARLY DRAFT OF LYRICS

I Cry Too

Something's wrong
She was lying on the bed
Crying, when I walked in and said
"you look like you're dying"
She said "I feel it
I've felt this way a long time"
Now she's gone

Later on
I would lie by her heart
Silent, but awake in the dark
The two of us staring
I thought "I've lost her
I loved her for a long time"
And now she's gone

It got so hard
It gets so hard
There's a feeling inside
That can't be described
It's not a question of death
Nor a matter of life
More a slow breaking down
Like emotional rust
It's an empty despair
That turns things to dust

And
Baby, baby
The whole world dies
So we die slowly
Darling, darling
I see you cry
So I cry with you too

Coming home
I would find her by the phone
Leaving her alone when it rang
But she never answered
Oh but I watched her
Her face shone like an angel
How it shone.

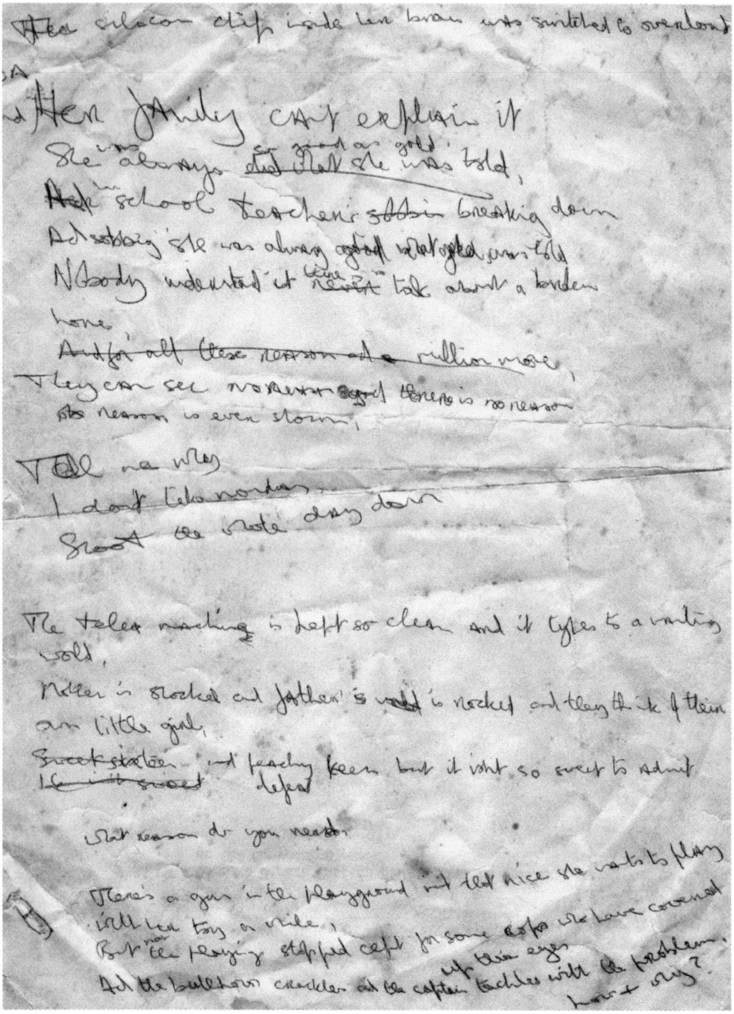

I Don't Like Mondays

The silicon chip inside her head
Gets switched to overload
And nobody's going to go to school today
She's gonna make them stay at home
And daddy doesn't understand it
He always said she was good as gold
And he can see no reason
Cos there are no reasons
What reasons do you need to be shown

Tell me why
I don't like Mondays
I want to shoot
The whole day down

The telex machine is kept so clean
And it types to a waiting world.
And Mother feels so shocked
Father's world is rocked
And their thoughts turn to
Their own little girl
Sweet 16 ain't that peachy keen
But it ain't so neat to admit defeat,
They can see no reasons
Cos there are no reasons
What reasons do you need to be shown

All the playing's stopped in the playground now
She wants to play with her toys awhile
And school's out early and soon we'll be learning
That the lesson today is how to die
And then the bullhorn crackles
And the captain tackles
With the problems and the how's and why's
And he can see no reasons
Cos there are no reasons
What reasons do you need to die?

Eva Braun

Sunday morning, Barwell Court, Chessington, Surrey. Paula brought the breakfast to bed. She was reading the News of the World and I had the Sunday Times. Some of the band were up already, you could hear the doors close and the moving about the house, the flushing loos and through the walls the muffled conversations as the other guys – the band, the crew – tried to remember what the girl's name was from the blurred or bleary hours of the previous Saturday night. The girls – indignant or uncaring and awkward round the other girlfriends or Gerry's wife – gradually trooped off to the station, wobbly in their suddenly silly Saturday night clothes and improbable Sunday morning heels. They gamely negotiated the gravel drive or waited for the mini-cab that the more considerate of the residents had ordered for them.

We all shared the house. It was a bit like being in a sort of deviant Monkees' film. The 6 band members, the manager, the 3 crew members, various girlfriends and a wife all billeted on the edge of London in a large country 'mansion' built directly alongside a zoo. At times it would have been difficult to distinguish between the zoo and the house and its inhabitants.

We were almost rock stars. First records and an album in the Top 20, selling out everywhere, Top Of The Pops, a beautiful funny, smart girlfriend. 18 months from Go to Boom!!! The dole office was a long 18 months past.

We took the house because of money, because we knew no one in huge London, because we were Irish in England and could stick together (and in the sticking bonded even closer) and because it had a big old ballroom where we could wake, breakfast, play. It was a gang house. And some really good songs and music came out of that place …

I was looking at the cover of the Sunday Times colour supplement. It was an old colour photo of an average girl in her bloom, in her one-piece swimsuit, stretching and smiling at the camera beside a lake. I recognised her, of course. It was Hitler's babe, Eva Braun. I looked at the other photos inside. More exercises and utter innocence on her face and trying to be beautiful and feminine and sexy for her man.

So far so normal. Except of course it was perverse beyond any rational recognisable version of what may constitute the norm. She was clearly in love and there is every evidence that this continued until their Wagnerian ending. But how is that possible? Shagging Hitler??? WTF will suffice here.

Was he a sweetie to her? A little cuddly bunny fluff in private? Her little Adolfy-poos dans la chambre? This vile, ascetic, shit-haircut, comedy-moustachioed, hali-toxic bore. This monotonous, mad, humourless, anti-life creep. How did this thing work?

I promise you that's what I felt and was thinking that morning – staring, really, actually staring at those sweet, 'gemütlichkeit' photos with an immense sadness for this deluded young woman. And what I thought was that it was so very sad because how did she not know that the man she had shackled her emotional life to was utterly and entirely incapable of empathy, that defining meta-characteristic of what it is to be human.

He was and – in history and forever – is the definition of the anti-human. Not the anti-Christ – spare me the spurious religious/mythic overtones, they're not needed here. The brute, stark reality that we must contend with and the most frightening thing of all, is that he was just another man. That is all. Not Beelzebub, not Lucifer, not sulphurous in any way, except for the stinking breath apparently.

He could empathise with nothing, save a dog. He appeared to appreciate children. But only in that suspect, over-jovial, heavy handed lap avuncular way. And of course, it was always other people's children. Far too self-absorbed to conceive of having his own. Besides, weren't ALL Germany's children his? And they, of course, would all adore him in return. What he displayed was a mawkish, kitsch sentimentalism towards children, a sort of retarded, pantomime emotion. You can't do that with your own brood. There's too much prosaic pragmatism involved with kids, the party frocks are only out on birthdays. Otherwise it's nappies, baby-grows and homework. Good ol' Unkel A. Dogs and other people's kids. I wouldn't have let the cunt come anywhere near mine.

Poor Eva, her little Swastikat was incapable of Love.

How annoying Eva must have been. In love, blathering on about going to the lake with the girls to do their aerobics and how she was now going for three lengths of the lake and she might be able to get there if she practised enough but she'd keep him updated and anyway she was off to the village to meet Magda for tea this avo and did he want her to get him some of those Sachertorte she knew he loved so much and there was absolutely zero animal products in them because she'd specifically asked the girl in the Konditorei and she had SWORN there was absolutely no animal products in them cos she knew he hated that and... SHUT UP bitch, I got some invadin' to do here!!!

Hitler's greatest horror-enabling tragedy, and therefore all of humanity's by default, was that he could not love. If one cannot love, one cannot understand what it is to be human. One cannot possibly understand Life. And how convenient that must be when one conjures up mad notions of organised industrial mass murder.

I scribbled his denial of his silly Mädchen on the back of the mag, picked up the guitar and worked out the tune.

(Also ref. 'To Live In Love'.)

Eva Braun

I never loved Eva Braun (oh no)
No, a 1000 people say I did, (oh yeah)
She was just some girl who was on everyone (yes we see)
Boy she wanted to be so big.
And in the end it got to be a drag
She's doing her exercises every day.
No matter what people say
I never loved Eva Braun.

I never heard the screams,
I never saw the blood and dirt and gore,
That wasn't part of the dream,
Of maps and generals and uniforms.
I'd always liked the big parade.
I always wanted to be adored,
In '33 I knew I had it made,
I never loved

Eva Braun wasn't history
She wasn't really part of my destiny
She never even fitted in the scheme of things,
She was a triumph of my will.
Oh yeah —
      the blondes with the blue eyes
I only saw the tanks and guns and planes.
I saw the millions saluting me,
Underneath I was really gentle,
Did you even see me touch a scrap of meat.
Well yes I conquered countries
Suppose we weren't it was strong
A little too ambitious maybe, but I never loved Eva Braun

BOB GELDOF

(I Never Loved) Eva Braun

I never loved Eva Braun (Oh no?)
No, a thousand people say I did (Oh yeah?)
Yeah, she was just some girl who was on the make (Yes, we see)
Boy, she wanted to be so big,
And in the end it got to be a drag,
She's doing her exercises every day,
No matter what people say,
I never loved Eva Braun

I never heard all the screams (Oh no?)
I never saw the blood and dirt and gore (Oh yeah?)
That wasn't part of the dream, (Yes, we see)
Of maps and generals and uniforms.
I'd always liked the big parade,
I always wanted to be adored,
In '33 I knew I had it made
But I never loved Eva Braun

Eva Braun wasn't history
She wasn't even part of my destiny
She never really fitted in the scheme of things
She was a triumph of my will
Oh yeah

I saw the blondies and the blue eyes, (Oh yeah?)
I saw the millions mouthing me, (Oh yeah?)
But underneath I was really gentle, (Oh yeah?)
Dja ever see me touch a scrap of meat?
O yeah I conquered all those countries
They were weak an' I was strong,
A little too ambitious maybe,
But I never loved Eva Braun,

Gee!

I Want You

I want you
I want you
I need you
I'll have you
And I'll have you
When I want to
Cos I need you
When I take you
And I'll take you
I'll take you
I need to
Have you
And I'll have you
When I want to
And if I want to
Then I'll take you

Cos I hate you
I hate you
And I hate you
Cos I love you
And I love you
I love you
And I want you
Cos I love you

And that's all I want to say
When I come home from work each day
Kick off my shoes kick back
And crack a beer
What do you want me to do?
What do you want me to say?
I can only say
I love you

'Get off your arse and make some tea
For once in your life
Do something nice for me'

BOB GELDOF

(I love you baby)

I want you
I want you
I need you
I'll have you
And I'll have you
When I want to
When I want to
I take you
And I take you
When I need to
And I'll have you
Cos I hate you
And I hate you
I hate you
And I'll take you
Cos I love you

That's all I wanna say
When I come home from work each day
Kick off my shoes kick back
And I'll crack a beer
There's no use looking at me
What you get is what you see
What else do you want me to say

'Get off your arse and make some tea
For once in your life
Do something nice for me'
(I'm listening baby)
(I hear you baby)
(*But you love me don't you baby*)
(*I love you baby*)
I want you

In The Pouring Rain

Everybody's gonna catch their death
In the pouring rain
Everybody better hold their breath
In the pouring rain
Everybody's gonna walk on by
Everybody hide away
Everybody's gonna pull their blinds
And stay inside and pass these days
I know I've seen a lot
Lord knows sometimes I've cried
But I know we can't sit like this
And shake our fists
While lovers kiss and die
In the pouring rain

I was hungry and I'm hungry still
And now it's pouring rain
I look o.k. but I've been feeling ill
And now it's pouring rain
Well hush now baby don't you cry
Tears won't wipe away the pain
There's a storm been blowing through the night
That's washed us down with lethal rain
Sometimes this world's too big
Sometimes we feel too small
Sometimes you'll have to pick me up
When I grow tired
Stumble, trip and fall
In the pouring rain

I'm gonna walk on by
Don't wanna see you cry
I'm gonna walk on by
In the pouring rain

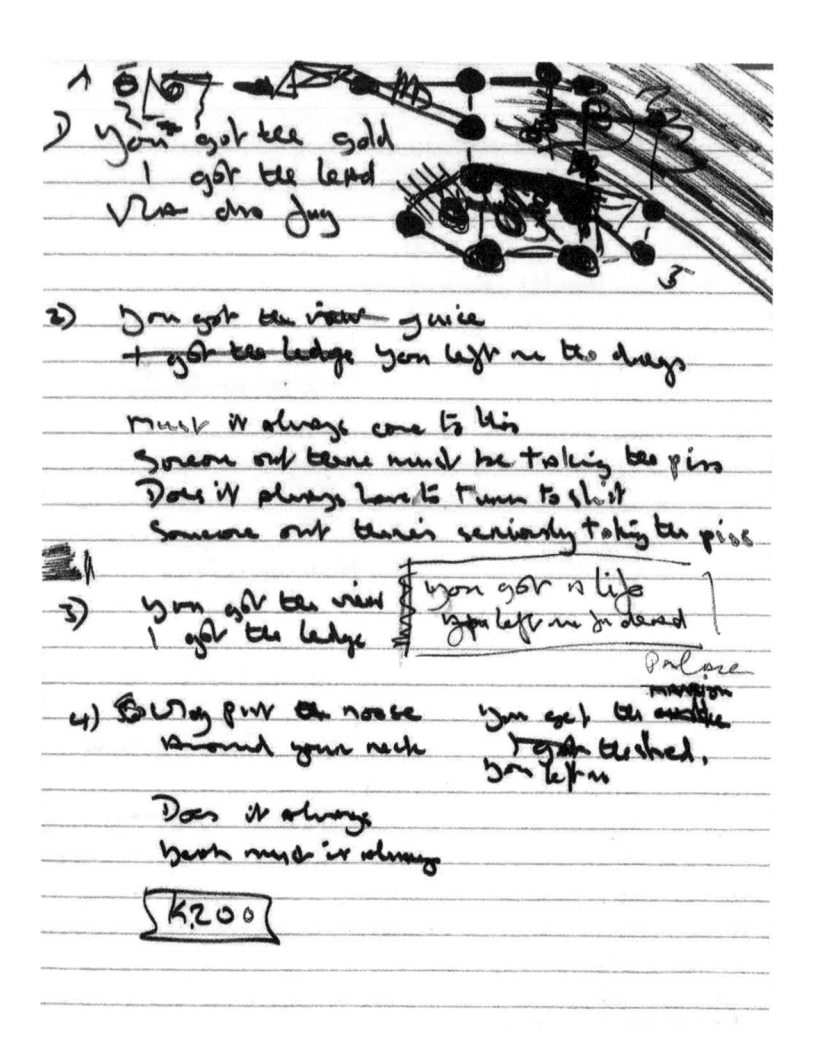

'INSIDE YOUR HEAD' DRAFT OF LYRICS

Inside Your Head

You got the gold, I got the lead
What the fuck's going on
Inside your head

You got the juice, you left me the dregs
What the fuck's going on
Inside your head

Must it always come to this
Someone out there
Must be taking the piss
Does it always have to
Turn to shit
Someone out there's
Seriously taking the piss

You got the view, I got the ledge
What the fuck's going on
Inside your head

You got the palace, you left me the shed
What the fuck's going on
Inside your head

You got a life, you left me for dead
What the fuck's going on
Inside your head

So why put a noose around your neck
What the fuck's going on
Inside your head

BOB GELDOF

It Doesn't Have To Be That Way

You told me to go 'way
You said you'd nothing more
I felt the sky give way
It doesn't have to be that way

Outside the light had faded
In those dying corpse of days
In the hallway hung the coats
Empty of their human shape

The best of us is love
The rest of us is dirt
So I wallow in the thickest mud
Those ponds of self-disgust

I did not love but yearned to love
I could not love but learned
Hard fought lessons at the hearts hot forge
Where learning I got burned

One day I'll wake up
Without those Morbid Blues
I'd stop eating dirt
Like I'm kissing earth
Baby you don't live on hallowed ground
Yes I could scrape that mud from off my shoes I could run amok
But if I may say
It doesn't have to be that way

I broke into the haunted house
And its abandoned empty rooms
And the abandoned empty lives that once
Occupied its ruin
And as the day grew older
I lit a fire in the gloom
And I spent another night with

The ghosts of me and you
Yes I broke into the haunted house
But I only heard my voice
Reflected back from all those tired lives
That once had had no choice

My holy Muslim brother
And my godlike Christian friends
And my fellow hollow atheists
We have nothing to defend
Our delusions are the best of us
While the rest us is maimed
And those imaginary lives we lead
That love has rendered lame

O my tired Muslim cousins
And my confused and Christian babe
My fellow godlike atheists
We have surrendered all the same
The dance of armies drunk on god
Will bring us to the brink
But nothing that those killers do
Could ever make me down that drink

One day I'll wake up
Without these Morbid Blues
We'll stop eating dirt
Like we're kissing earth
We can live on hallowed ground
And yes if everything was equal
And there was no one left to blame
I'd still say, O.K.
But it doesn't have to be this way.

It's 3

I find these early songs and bits of juvenilia all over the place. And sometimes they still stir me. I remember this. I remember where and when and how I was when I wrote it. But I only remember because of these words. Otherwise that night and this girl would no more have existed then the other ten thousand moments of a life. It is spare and it is bleak, and it is still true. I think I also remember its spare, bleak 'melody'. A barely muttered, plucked 2-chord little bit of L. Cohen-ish blue. No need to explain it. It's as described. Exactly. A snapshot of self-pity, waiting and loss at 17.

It's 3

It's 3
Here's me
The fire's low
Like me

There's a bird outside
And I'm inside
Looking out
At the morning dawn.

I wonder is it worth going to bed at all
And would I fall asleep without you beside me

I'll make myself another cup of tea
One spoon for the pot
One spoon for me

BOB GELDOF

It's All The Rage

Everybody I meet wants to knock me down
A friend told me it's the new thing that's doing the rounds

It's all the rage
You're putting me on
A new craze
Is sweeping the town
A new way
Of keeping everybody down

They're out on the streets
They're using their feet
A bloody face is worth a laugh or two
They use their fists these days

You took the risk and you opened up Pandora's box
Look what jumped out
Now someone's gone and stolen all the locks

Don't talk to me of teenage angst and burning fire
I don't believe it all excuses are the same
You're looking round for scapegoats everywhere you go
Look in the mirror and you'll know just who's to blame
Oi Oi

After getting punched in the face at the Music Machine, Camden 1977.

It's Been A Good Life

It's been a good life
I can't complain
I could have done with
A bit less pain
But if you want the rainbows
First you got to have the rain
It's been a real good life
It's been a good life
And now it's nearly done
It's funny how you get to be
What you've become
My father always told me
That I'd end up as a bum
(he was wrong)
It's been a real good life

It's been a good life
Let's raise a cheer
From how I got
From there to here
Let's pop a bottle of champagne
And a couple of crates of beer
To a real good life

I've crashed and burned and stumbled
But still I've fumbled through
Had hits and stiffs and smashes
Huge applause and bigger boos
But friends and family
Children, wives and lovers
Pulled me through
To a real good life
It's been a good life
And now my way is clear
Put that box up on your shoulders
And get me outta here
Let all the woman cry
And the guys can clap and cheer

BOB GELDOF

Goodbye, good luck
And thanks so much
I love you all my dears
It would have been nothing
Had all of you guys not been here
And given me those great fantastic
Wonderful, joyful, all amazing years
Of my Real Good LIFE!!!!

Sort of Frank Sinatra-ish but wobbles crazily at the end. Not in any way finished. I'll get back to it. Probably closer to the Finishing Line.

Joey

I tentatively explored how far we could go on those first songs and on the first TV shows.

These were songs of course about being young and its sidekick – sex. Boys: 'Kicks', Girls: 'Mary Of The Fourth Form', Me: 'My Blues Away'. Fuck the church. Songs about new ideas that had begun to circulate that made you question your own assumptions: 'Never Bite The Hand That Feeds'. About falling in love in the time of killing: 'I Can Make It (If You Can)'. About a politician who appeared in England out of the blue and looked like she might be trouble: '(She's Gonna) Do You In'. There were others that never made it onto that first album and some of them are here, too. Then there is 'Joey'…

Joey was a gouger. A yahoo. Corner boy. Guttersnipe. Young hooligan. He did drugs. I heard he sold them. Before they found his body somewhere down around the Pigeon House cooling stacks he had come to a good few Rats' shows down in the basement of the hotel we played fairly regularly, in a tough area on the north side of the city.

Dublin divides in two. Posh, south of the river. Poor, north. Least it did back then. It's a big gang's town. We were middle-class boys from the southside determined to mess things up. Maybe that was why the first kids who took to us were from around the tenements and estates of the Five Lamps, Sheriff St., Gardiner St. and the rest. Gloomtown Rats.

He never went nuts at the gigs. It was because he just stared at us that I noticed him. The basement was tiny. A bar, small stage, hundred, hundred and fifty people max. Couldn't help but see him standing over to the side, always to my right, half-hidden behind the pillar that Phil Lynott used to loll lazily, sexily against when he would come checking us out.

What age was Joey? Skinny, tight-faced and gaunt. Wiry and often wired by the looks of him. Maybe a junkie. I suppose so, how else would he feed his habit other than by selling the stuff? Then they have you. 19? Younger maybe.

We knew something was happening around the band when we arrived early for the gig. A queue stretched up Gardiner St. We were amazed. Nobody ever queued for a local band. I'd never seen one. You just pitched up when you felt like it. The gigs were never full really, it was all so annoyingly casual. Not at all rock 'n' roll and no pretence towards it. It was all about your competence. Who the fuck cares how well you can play? It's what and how you play … What's the attitude of the band and how that translates to the noise they make. Joey must have liked the noise. And the others, waiting in line 90 minutes before showtime.

I was in the bar on the ground floor. I looked out at the punters going down outside to the basement – The Much More Music Gig at Morans Hotel. Joey wasn't in the queue. Instead he just arrived at the front of the line and waved a drumstick at the bouncer who nodded him through. After the gig I asked the bouncer who the kid was. "Whaddyeh thalkin' 'bow'?" he said. The kid with the drumstick? "He's yoo-er fuggin' thrummer inntee!" Looking at me with disgust. No. No he's not. "Wha?" sez yer man, the light dawning. "Tha' cheeky fugger. Fuggin nex thoy-em oi see him…"

Then we heard he was dead. Probably killed. Wasn't surprised really. Nobody was. He wasn't a friend. But he could stay alive in the song long enough to tell the story of that hopeless lost life. No romance.

There just wasn't any romance or hope in our town. The very opposite of a boomtown. An additional irony to the name I suppose. There would be two other 'Dublin' songs – 'Rat Trap' and 'When The Night Comes'.

A trilogy of hopelessness.

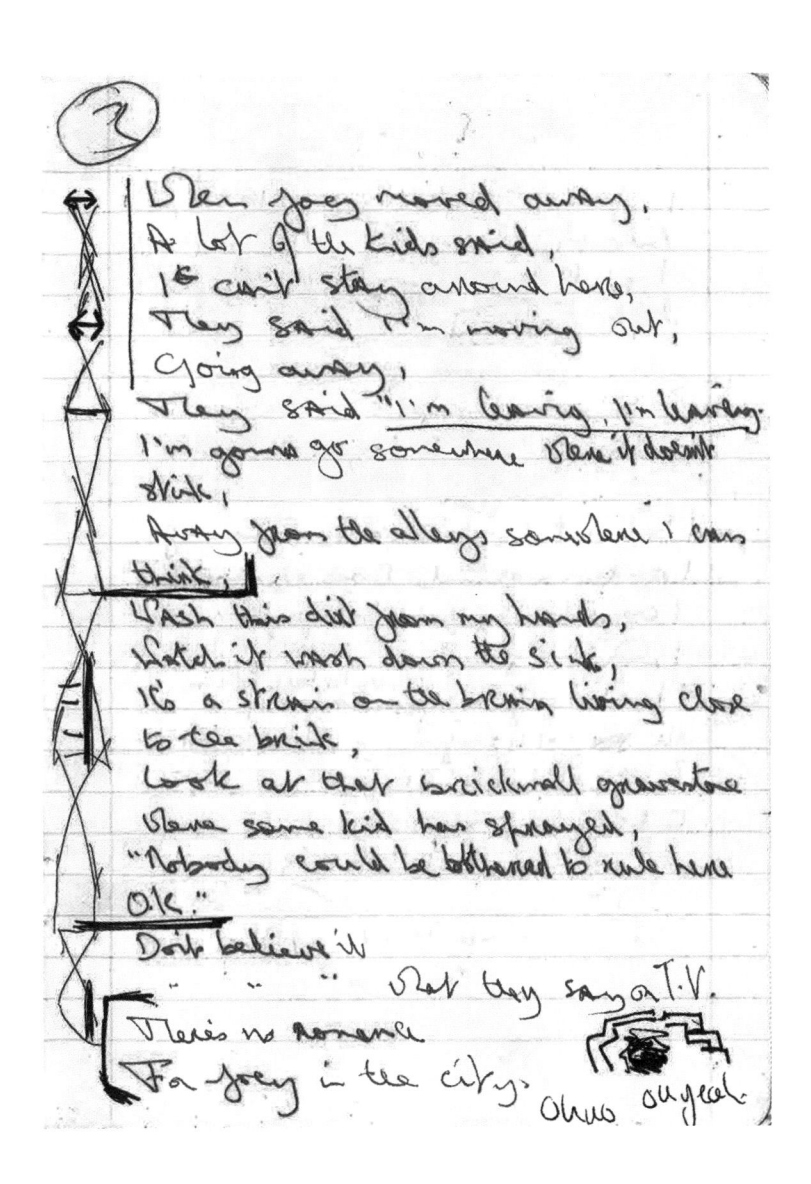

When Joey moved away,
A lot of the kids said,
I can't stay around here,
They said I'm moving out,
Going away,
They said "I'm leaving, I'm leaving.
I'm gonna go somewhere where it doesn't
stink,
Away from the alleys somewhere I can
think,
Wash this dirt from my hands,
Watch it wash down the sink,
It's a strain on the brain living close
to the brink,
Look at that brickwall gravestone
where some kid has sprayed,
"Nobody could be bothered to rule here
O.K."
Don't believe it
" " " what they say on T.V.
There is no romance
For Joey in the city. Ohno oh yeah

BOB GELDOF

Joey's On The Streets Again

Sooner or later when the dawn was breaking
The joint was jumping and the walls were shaking
Joey sneaked in the backdoor way
Pretending he was with the band, he never used to pay
He was no great draw at pulling the chicks
He used to lie against the wall like he was holding up the bricks
And all the things that guy used to do to get his kicks
He was a legend in his lifetime with the neighbourhood kids

They said "Joey did this" and "Joey did that"
Oh that guy was crazy, what a crazy cat
Then something strange would happen, there's trouble
    on the way
And trouble only means one thing...
Joey's on the street again.

Joey grew older, older without a cause
Got married, had some kids and had his brushes with the law
Settled down and got a job, then said "I'm leaving" one day
"I've gotta hang loose a while, take care while I'm away."
People said they'd seen him, they were nearly always wrong
No one knew how much he had, where he'd gone or for
    how long
'Til one day there came a rumour, floating from the docks
Saying a crazy stranger had been found lying among the rocks.

They said "Joey was this" and "Joey was that"
Oh that guy was crazy, what a crazy cat
But no one quite believed it, all rumours are the same
And now if something happens they say...
Joey's on the street again.

When Joey moved away
A lot of the kids said "I can't stay around here"
They said "I'm moving out, going away"
They said "I'm leaving, getting out"
"I'm gonna go somewhere where it doesn't stink
Away from the alleys, somewhere I can think

THE BOOMTOWN RATS, 1977

Wash the dirt from my hands, watch it wash down the sink
It's a strain on the brain living close to the brink"

Look at that brickwall gravestone where some kid has sprayed
Saying "Nobody could be bothered to rule O.K."
Don't believe it, don't believe it what they say on TV
There's no romance, no romance
For Joey in this city.

BOB GELDOF

Johnny Nogood

Here comes Johnny Nogood
With his twisted smile
And his brain full of horror
And his mouth full of bile
Fraying threads still cling him
To some shred of sanity
But Johnny's too involved
In his own reality

"o Johnny I so love you"
She says at his blank gaze
His mind goes blank
His hair hangs lank
Round Johnny's pale blank face

Later after soaking
All the blood up off the floor
He eats the meal she made him
And then gently
Shuts the door

Just Get On

I thought I'd write a letter
Tell you how it's goin'
Everything's a little better
We thought you'd like to know

Everyone's a little bigger
Even in so short a space of time
But then some unseen vicious trigger
Can start them all to crying

And you know you just get on with it
You know you just go on

And the feeling that it's hopeless
Gets so huge it overwhelms
But as we crawl through every hour
So the days go 'round again
And I look at all their little heads
So full of lice and pain
And I wonder if you knew just what you did
Would you still do it just the same

But you know you just get on with it
You know you just get on

And if you think that I sound desperate
Man you should have heard the other songs
It's just that my weary soul gets restless
From the peace I know
That must come along

And you know you just get on with it
You know you just get on
And on and on and on and on
But don't get me wrong
You can never be that strong
So you just get on with it

BOB GELDOF

Keep It Up

In her £2.00 coat
She really thinks she's cloaked in mystery
She's acting like some character from Agatha Christie
I got a pain in my shoes and all I wanna do is dance

I can remember those carefully sharpened eyeballs
Sparkling like bloodshot diamonds in the snowfall
She always said she thinks she knows where things
    are roughly at
Well maybe she does, but then she says

Does it feel nice – does it feel right, does it feel alright
Does it feel good, (quite nice)
Can you keep it up, can you keep it up – upright
Does it let you down, I heard it lets you down – sometimes

Snap me in your breach, I want to be your bullet
I want a little kiss that's gonna take my breath away
And every lover tries to do things in a different way
That's what they all say

K.I.S.S.

With a kiss
With a kiss
With a gut-wrench flip
It's a hit on the lips
It's a k.i.s.s.

With a tongue in my lung
It's fun
Gonna cum and then run
With a k.i.s.s.

Soul take a stroll
Gotta be a love mole
Digging in that hole
For a k.i.s.s.

At the end of the world
At the final twirl
Gonna find me a girl
For a k.i.s.s.

Don't shut your mouth
Just let it out
Ya gotta scream and shout
From way down south
(from your guts down south)

All night
Big fight
Baby make it alright
I'm a sucker for a pucker
Of a k.i.s.s.

Ripped out
Tripped out
DJ give a shout out
Riffing on a pout mouth
K.i.s.s.

BOB GELDOF

Hip to the groove
'N your hips start to move
Slip into the mood
Of a k.i.s.s.

It's a bottomless pit
It's a cliff, the abyss
It's hell, it's bliss
It's a k.i.s.s.

Don't shut your mouth
Just let it out
You gotta scream and shout
From your guts down south

K.I.S.S.

N.B. *If you've got this track you'll know there's a "Rap" in it. But the Rap doesn't make any sense. We just wanted the sound of it. So Pete downloaded a jive rap that sounded good, cut it up and stuck it in. Unbelievably, it has the words "The clasp of a Rat" in it. Spooky.*

Kicks

I don't get my kicks no more from cake or lemonade
And I can't get served no smokes or drinks
They tell me that I'm underage

At sixteen years old I don't stand a chance
But on Saturday when I get to the dance
It's time-out from life
Got to learn to boogaloo
'Cos I get my kicks from you

Summer's gone, school's back I feel so black inside
Rules and regulations are a torture rack
Is there no place for me left to hide?

At sixteen years old things have gone too far
I wanna be a movie, rock or soccer star
But when you're around I know you'll treat me good
And I get my kicks from you

I dream of you at night
Do you mean anything at all,
Or am I wasting my time on you?

Those other guys are so much cooler than me
I find it so hard to score
What's it really like to know a girl?
My imagination's not enough I gotta know more

At sixteen years old I get frightened at night
Presented with the truth I'm afraid I take fright
But you don't mess with my head
When I'm with you things are cool
I get my kicks from you
I get my kicks from you

BOB GELDOF

Late Last Night

Were you really frightened
Cos I heard you late last night
You were screaming
Were you dreaming
Is it okay?
It's all right
Oh no must be something I ate
Late last night

There's terror in the shadows
And there's horror in the night
I don't like it in the dark
And I'm not so sure about the light
Oh no it must be something I ate
late last night

Late last night
I heard the madness stir inside my brain
Late last night
I was calm I couldn't take the strain
Late last night I never want to hear that sound again

I'm falling and I'm spinning
And I'm dying in my dreams
And the flies are sucking at my sores
I'm leaking at the seams
Oh no it must be something I ate
late last night

Is it something I said
Is it something you'd die for
Swill a stick around my head
Inside it's always black
and brown

I see white rooms
I see white tiles
White roofs and pure white walls

And there's a neon strip of icy blue
that's shining in the hall,
and then the blood
the blood starts seeping
Through the ventilator screen
It's dribbling from behind the wall
And soon I hear the screams.
Oh no it must be something I ate
late last night

BOB GELDOF

Let It Go

My friend she's on fire
She's burning like a juniper tree
She don't know what to do
But I do
'Cause she do it to me
Let it go let it go

It's not nice to be like ice
It's much better if you feel like fire
Yes there's a bad moon coming up
And I can see it's on the cusp
Electric winds are shrieking up in the wires
But it's a warm evening out
It feels like New Orleans blue
On the spray from the African shore
Oh we could make it coast to coast
She said "ain't that the most"
But I could tell she'd heard it all before
Let it go let it go
Let it shine down on me

Is this a love affair or is this a crime
Is this religion without priests, prayers or pews
This is the view from the left-over shelf
This is the punchline and the joke's on you
I don't need her kissy lips
I don't need her armies or her pearls
I fell asleep and dreamed of far off lands
When I awoke I nearly married that girl
Let it go let it go

Life Is The Hardest Thing

Life is the hardest thing
It's the hardest thing
The hardest thing
To do it
And if you do it
You live through it
And that's called 'being human'
Yea life is the hardest thing to do

Give us all a smile now
Stay with us a while now
Hold us tight don't let us go
Cos well you know
That life is the hardest thing to do

It begins and ends and
The question is what then and
The only thing that bothers me
Is when?
Til then
Life is the hardest thing to do

BOB GELDOF

Like Clockwork

I'm not disconnected
I'm not unaware,
I'm in one place at one time,
I'm neither here nor there,
I'm hooked to the mainstream,
Tuned into the world,
Plugged into my surroundings,
Not out on a limb.
I'm thinking in a straight line,
I'm thinking that these thoughts are mine,
My heart is beating oh-so-fast
I feel the hours crashing
Because my mind keeps time like clockwork,
And I think in sync like clockwork.

She's done away with emotion,
She sees things clearly now,
She says she sees it all from her room,
And it looks so small from her room,
It's alright, it's alright,
I'm on your side...... for a while,
She thinks time is a concept by which we measure our pain
(She'll say it again)
She wants to say it again, but she doesn't have time,
And now her heart beats time like clockwork
And she thinks in sync like clockwork.

Count the hours, count the months and minutes,
You're born in tears and you die in pain and that's your limit
You're lookin' for a reason but there's none there,
Why don't you admit it
We'll make the most of what we've got, that's the ticket
My, my, my.

I stayed in that room a long, long time
And watched the seasons gliding past
And hey... what's the matter?
We've got time, lots of time,

It's alright, it's alright,
I'm on your side for a while,
We'll wind up
We'll slow down
We'll speed up, move around and we'll maybe overwind...
But now our minds beat time
Like clockwork

BOB GELDOF

Like Down On Me

She takes her face off
And she puts it in a row
Upon the shelf
It's where she keeps the bottles
Of the essence of herself
Sometimes she takes them down
And shakes them
When she finds herself in deep despair
Then the voodoo of the suburbs
Comes around
And fixes up her hair. Yep.

Like down on me

She keeps a raven in the hole of her guitar
And when she feeds him then it plays a sad song
That would melt the coldest heart
Sometimes she strums the strings with it
And then it bites her fingers
And it sucks the blood from off the strings
Before it disappears again. Yep.

Like down on me

5 seconds later
In the out-of-work elevator
She calls room service for some air
They pump it in, but it's not fair
With bell-boys, bell-hops call 'em what you like to
But they're gasping for a lungful which they feel they have a right to
You could tell by the light as it flickered off/on
It was a major-like emergency with all the knobs on
Call a paramedic with a first-aid kit
And a third class brain and for God's sake be quick
And just as everybody starts to hyperventilatin'
The whole thing starts to shake and
resume its elevatin'. Yep.

BOB GELDOF

Later on that evening
When the snow had fallen
The girls were calling
She slips on her raincoat
Of the finest woven green tarpaulin
She put a bunch of worms into the hole of her guitar
For the raven if he needs to eat they're going pretty far
And just before she packs it in its plastic carry case
He pokes his battered beak out and drops
The diamond necklace
He'd stolen just the day before from the jar
Which hold her neck and face like a jewelled star
Stop that, she said look at what you've done
But it played a pretty song 'cos it was overcome
By the light of the moon and the way it shone
As it glittered on the E-string which was highly strung
So they make it, wading through the melting ice
When they got there, it's hot there everybody was nice
She told a stupid joke and she felt like a fool
And they said how's the bird and from its hole it said
I'm cool. Yep.

BOB GELDOF

The Little Death

"So I turned on the radio and everyone was listening
to chicken jazz"

See that man over there...
He's got cold feet
He'd march to the drum
But the drummer's
Dead beat
He's fragile tonight
But he says he's clean
He's uncertain when he's speaking
But he knows what he means
Ah he's shivering now
But he don't look cold
He say
Turn up the weather
So I do as I'm told
Do you know about empty
Die a little inside
Cos he hasn't lived until he's died
You couldn't have lived until you've tried
He hasn't lived until he's died
The Little Death

See that woman over there
She got cold feet
She'd march to the drum
But the drummer's
Dead beat
She reach for the sky
But the sky turn black
She hanging by her nails
But her knuckles just cracked
She said, "It's strange but nice to have no
future or past
If you can't stand the heat
you just turn up the gas"

200   **V DEEP, 1982**

I nod as if I know she can't say I haven't tried
Cos she hasn't lived until she's died
you couldn't have lived until you've tried
She hasn't lived until she's died
The Little Death

BOB GELDOF

Living In An Island

Night fell fast, like it did in the past
When the phone rang twice and a voice
Said "I think I'm alone"
I gave my advice
And the voice said "Nice,
But suicide leaves such a bad
Aftertaste on the soul"

Oh ain't you glad that we live in an island,
You can choose your own way of being killed,
You can jump off a cliff and get drowned in the sea,
Or be dashed 'gainst the rocks and get split,
And it could happen to you (no it won't happen to me)
Yeah, it could happen to you...
...And if it do then you're a true blue sui...

...Side by side they walked into the tide,
Till it rose to their nose
And then they kissed with their eyes "goodbye"
They were seen to smile
Just before they dived,
Dead lovers don't have much
Except a certain desperate sense of style...

But ain't you glad that you live on an island

There were a lot of crazy problems that they couldn't resolve
A lot of tricky questions which they just couldn't solve
The main problem was of course he couldn't say "no"
On your marks, get ready, steady here we go.

In a fifth floor lift a man slit his wrist,
His head ticked over and then
It suddenly slipped away
And the girl in the mac
At the back of the shack,
Lay her head on the track
And said "I think it's better this way"

Oh she was glad that she lived on an island

Lookin' After No. 1

But then we hit our stride.

In November '75 I was standing in line in the queue outside the dole office on Georges St., Dun Laoghaire (pron. 'leery'). It was November. Cold. East wind. Sleet rain and a line of roughly middle-aged men who through no fault of their own had no jobs. The office was meant to open at 9am. Outside we huddled and stamped. 9am came and went. Inside in the cosy paraffin stove heated, brass-barred room I imagined these indifferent civil servants, soft in their sinecures, guaranteed pensions, cradling warm mugs of tea in their bleak, pale green and dirty cream surroundings of governmental well-being. Superior. They had jobs. Let the lumpen proles wait. A bit of cold will sharpen them up anyway. "Make them get a job, lazy fuckers ..." THERE ARE NO JOBS. THE COUNTRY HAS BEEN FUCKED OVER AGAIN. FUCK YOU, OPEN THE DOOR. GIVE ME MY MONEY!!!! That was in my head y'unnerstan'. I borrowed a pencil that was in the ear of the man in front of me. He used it for marking that day's races on the Racing Post, but was now using the sodden rag to try and keep the biting rain off his oily head. On my unemployment card I scrawled 'The world OWES me a living/I've waited on this dole queue too long/Standing in the rain 15 minutes/That's a quarter of an hour TOO LONG?/I'm not going to be like you/I'm GOING TO BE ME!!!'

Turned out to be, with the odd change for scansion purposes, the first thing most people heard me and the Rats say.

Now we and I were off and running.

April 1973

19 Thursday

The world owes me a living
I bin waiting on this dole queue too long,
I bin waiting here for 15 minutes
An' that's a quarter of an hour too long,
I don't want no dead-end job
~~Someone~~ telling me how life should be run,
I told my ol' man an' ol' lady,
I'm grown up now, I can do what I want.
I told them.
Take your money
Count your losses and run
Your investment pulling out,
He's gonna get him some fun.

20 Friday
Good Friday

The man in the government told me,
He's got a new programme for people like you,
He really understood how hard it is,
For unemployed lads just after leaving school
I said man you've gotta be crazy,
At last I got a life of my own
You bastards owe me a living
I'm running just ad I'm going strong
I told him

Lookin' After No. 1

The world owes me a living
I've waited on this dole queue too long
I've been standin' in the rain for fifteen minutes
An' that's a quarter of an hour too long.

I'll take all they can give me
And then I'm gonna ask for more
Cos the money's buried deep in the Bank of England
And I want the key to the vault

I'm gonna take your money
Count your loss when I'm gone.
I'm all right, Jack,
I'm lookin' after number one.

If I want something I get it
Don't matter what I have to do
I'll step on your face, or your mother's grave
Never underestimate me I'm nobody's fool

I don't owe nobody nothing
Cos it's me that must come through
Why don't you stop, think, look, babe
I always get what I want and I wanna get you

I don't wanna be like you.
I don't wanna live like you.
I don't wanna talk like you.

Don't give me "love thy neighbour"
Don't give me charity
Don't give me "peace and love" or "the good lord above"
You only get in my way with your stupid ideas

BOB GELDOF

I am an island
Entire of myself
And when I get old, older than today
I'll never need anybody's help in any way.

I'm gonna be like
I'm gonna be like
I'm gonna be like ME

Love Like A Rocket

Obviously, I love The Kinks. Who doesn't? If you're interested in the great pop song writers, then you put Ray Davies on that Olympic stage. 'Waterloo Sunset' is simply too brilliant. I don't know if you like poems, but there have been some great ones about London. London, the most exciting city in the world and my favourite.

In school we had to learn 'Upon Westminster Bridge'. I always imagined Wordsworth wandering home in the early dawn, maybe a bit pissed after a night out with the lads and as ever there were no tubes or buses at 4.30am. Yea, I know that they didn't *actually* exist then (FFS), I was just picturing it cos it's so good, that poem. Anyway, he's a bit knackered and sobering up (before he gets home and gets a bollocking from Dorothy, his devoted sister, "Where the hell have you been William ... eh? That's it ... it's off to the Lake District for us ... I'm not having you ..." etc.) and the sun is coming up over the river and it takes his breath away. The beauty and the drink and the walk pull him up sharp and he takes a minute to put his elbows on the bridge and just ... look. The sky is purple, then pink and blue are just skimming the dome of St. Paul's. A river of gold rushes by beneath him and under the bridge the early morning air is sharp and fresh before the stinking sewer smell of the waking city plummets untreated into the golden river and the invigorating sharp dawn air. "Earth has not any thing to show more fair..." he thinks in wonder, staring awestruck at what nature and Man has wrought. The best is the end though: 'Dear God! The very houses seem asleep; And all that mighty heart is lying still!' Isn't that FANTASTIC?! London. That 'Mighty Heart' – and it really is.

My point is that between Wordsworth and Shelley's compelling and scabrous description of the same city and Ray Davies' 'Waterloo Sunset' (which is the 20th century Wordsworthian vision), I couldn't wait to get to the mighty heart of the action. Fuck Dun Laoghaire. 'Tired N Weary/Drab N Dreary/That's it Dun Laoghaire'). There's the boat. Here's my ticket. Outta there!!

Davies' song is so full of compelling imagery I could taste the city. I saw it in the same way I saw Wordsworth's images. But I always wondered what happened to the two protagonists in Ray's song. We know that Terry met Julie every Friday night at the tube station but what happened to them? I conjured them up again and wrote down what I imagined became the rest of their lives.

It turned out that they loved each other still, but the disappointments of an every day normality that must follow the optimism and idealism of being young and in love could not be turned round by their romantic Friday evening tradition of meeting each other upon Waterloo Bridge at sunset and quietly holding hands. They watched the sun sink and the river, like their lives, flow steadily, inevitably, monotonously by beneath them.

Of course, my song – i.e. the story of Terry and Julie that I called 'Love Like A Rocket' – is not even within 53 light years of Davies' genius, beautiful thing. Rather it's a workmanlike exercise in prosaic story-telling. It just resolves a cycle that started for me when I was 14 but I apologise to Ray for the inadequacy of my effort and hope it has not spoilt or besmirched the wonder of his perfect song.

Love Like A Rocket

Terry still meets Julie every Friday night
Down at Waterloo underground
Nothing much has changed
Except now they're both afraid
But they're not sure what went wrong
Terry holds her tight and says
Some things I can't explain
But in twenty years baby
Some things have got to change
Paradise is gone
If it was ever on
But there's one thing Julie
That'll always be the same
My love like a rocket
Like a rocket on fire
Goes straight up to the sky
Love like a rocket
Like a rocket on fire
I'm gonna love you till the day I die
But Julie's not convinced that that's enough anymore
Cos the Waterloo sunset won't work for her anymore

Julie cries a lot but she tries to hide the tears
From the kids coming in from school
She's looking at a picture taken Margate '66
Of Terry on the pier looking cool
She tries to remember the boy in the snap
But the baby's woken up from her afternoon nap
She runs a wrinkled hand through her tired hair
Then sighs and mutters something sounding
close to despair
But love like a rocket
Like a rocket on fire
Goes straight up to the sky
He's gonna love her till the day he dies
But in the middle of another little household chore
She knows the Waterloo sunset won't work for her anymore

Standing on the bridge
Terry stops and checks his wrist
As the water rushes by below
It's almost half past six but the people moving by
Make it seem like twenty years ago
Julie gets there late but she always makes him wait
Until the sky turns from red to gold
She says "Terry I don't think we should
come here no more"
And like he's waited for this moment
He just stares and says "I know"

And love like a rocket
Like a rocket on fire
Goes straight up to the sky
Love like a rocket
Like a rocket on fire
He'll love her till the day he dies
And then he squeezes Julie's hand
As the water starts to glow
A tear falls in the river and disappears with the flow
And is gone.

Love Or Something

It was last night baby when I caught your eye
Sssh don't tell nobody but I almost died
And like a beach bunny sobbing on a shag pile rug
I thought of "Going to a Go-Go"
And the Family Stone frug
So we twist and shout then when it's feeling great
She drifts away
(Talk talk baby whaddya say)
She walk away
(Walk walk baby why don't you stay)
But like a cardboard suitcase in the pouring rain
She falls apart on me and then we start again
It must be love
Or something else

Well I talk with her and then I stay all night
We did everything but it
Still it felt alright
She was careful 'bout her health so it didn't hurt
When she started dropping pills in her blue grass skirt
Then she twist and dip and do the flip-flop slide
She drifts away
(Talk talk baby whaddya say)
She walk away
(Walk walk baby why don't you stay)
Well trembling like an earthquake, slippin' like soap
I don't believe with her I'll ever give up hoping
This is love
Or something else
Still I never take for granted that what's new
Am I overstating what at root
Seems cute
And more to boot
The point is moot
But up to you
Is this love
Or something else

BOB GELDOF

I don't believe in love baby if I'm honest with myself
I don't believe it lasts long it's kinda like your health
Hey everything is spinning round down the laundromat
And love is like your clothes it's only useful while it lasts
Save your soul

Dans se monde il n'ya qu'une femme pour chaque homme
Et je pense qu'il n'ya qu'un age pour chaque age
Et ca c'est vraiment vrai

Lying Again

Here they go, lying again
Beating everybody at their favourite game
But in the end nobody wins

There they go let's pretend
The rules have changed but the name's the same
And in the end nobody wins no

Do you think they don't know what they're doing
Do you think they don't know who they're fooling

When I was a boy and I was told
That heaven was hot and hell was cold
If I told lies I'd freeze my soul
But it didn't seem to matter

There they go lying again
They want it just as much as us
And in the end nobody wins no

There they go lying again
They pulled the wool and we all fell in
And in the end nobody wins

MARY

Sitting in the front row,
Mary of the 4th form,
Turning all the boys on,
Turning all the heads around,
Hitching up her short skirt,
Stretching out her long legs,
Pulling up her stockings,
Combing out her black hair

Leave that kid alone, x3.

Mary's so different when she's not at home.

But in the middle of the night
She waits for mom to turn off the light,
Her make-up's on and her jeans are skintight
And she's headed for the Pillar Room.

She walks into the pool hall room.
The music's playing, you can see in the gloom,
The boys are lounging around Table No. 5.

Johnny looks alright tonight she thinks,
He gives her a smile and he buys her a drink,
Shoots off a game and they head off into the night.

PAGE × 2

Teacher's losing control
Thankfully the bell rings.
Mary's left all alone,
With no-one but the teacher,
She quietly drops her pencil,
And slowly bends to get it,
Teacher is a natural man
His hand moves out to touch her.

BOB GELDOF

Mary Of The Fourth Form

Sitting in the front row
Mary of the fourth form
Turning all the boys on
She's turning all the heads around

Hitching up her short skirt
Stretching out her long legs
Pulling up her stockings
She's combing out her black hair
Staring at the teacher
Opening her lips wide
Shifting in her seat. Yeah,
She slowly moves her hips aside

But in the middle of the night
She waits her Mom to put out the light
Her make-up's on and her jeans are skintight
And she's heading to the Pillar Bar
She walks into the pool room
The music's playing, you can see in the gloom
The boys are hangin' out around table number 5
Johnnie looks all right tonight she thinks
He gives her a smoke and he buys her a drink
He shoots off a frame and they head off into the night.

Teacher's losing control
Thankfully the bell rings
Mary's left all alone
With no one but the teacher
She quickly drops her pencil
And slowly bends to get it
Well, the teacher is a natural man
His hand moves out to touch her
She straightens and looks around, now
She laughs and leaves the room, yeah
Heartbreak for the teacher
And sweet dreams for young Mary

But in the middle of the night...

THE BOOMTOWN RATS, 1977

BOB GELDOF

Mary Says

Mary says she feels the Winter comin in
She sniffs the cooling air like some old dog
She says the problem with these endless summers
Is endless summers always have to end
She packs a pen inside an empty pocket
She says it's all she's ever going to need
"I'll write a book of poems if I go hungry"
She looks around just once before she leaves

Everybody's always saying goodbye
Everybody's got some place to leave
Goodbye, goodbye

Beheaded suns will light her crooked pathway
Six-pointed stars illuminate her road
Amputee moons guide her through her darkest nights
And silver armies help to ease her load
She says her problem with these endless summers
Is endless summers always have to end
The thinning sky is throwing loveless shadows
The Summer's gone and Autumn's almost spent

Goodbye, goodbye,
Everybody always says goodbye

Mary feels the Winter coming in
She smells it on the cooling breeze

Maybe Heaven

Why does this happen to me
I never know what's happening
It's 2am and the world has stopped
4am I've smoked til I dropped
Sometimes I believe that I'm in heaven

Why do you this to me
I should have seen it coming
Catch me loose
Soaked in gin
Feel this good
It must be a sin
If this is hell
Then baby I'm in heaven.

What's it doing
What's it doing to me

Why does she do this to me
I should have seen it happening
What I'm saying
I know is dumb
Gets this late
An' I feel numb
Baby sometimes
It's a sort of heaven

Whatcha doin'
Whatcha doin' to me

And I feel slow
But I'm not disturbed
Going to let tonight
Ripple round the world
Dream of pale and languid girls
Curled up round me
Yea, that's what I'll dream

BOB GELDOF

Hey! 5 o'clock
Hey! Check your watch
Get up
Get up
Your coach is on the call
Get out of the bed
And crawl motherfucker crawl

Why's this always happening to me
I should have seen it coming
I'm seeing things
And I don't know what
If you do too much
You'll lose the plot
Put this pilot
On a course for heaven

What's it doing
What's it doing to me

Me And Howard Hughes

Hand me down a strong panacea,
One that's guaranteed to make me feel like Hercules,
There's flies everywhere, buzzing in the air,
Filling my body with filth and disease... and I think,

He thinks he should develop a complex,
He thinks that he really owes it to himself,
His friends'll all say he's looking sick and unhealthy
An' then he can wallow in sweet self-neglect.

He's going to lock himself up in his room
Shutter the windows and bolt all the doors,
Wrap himself round in his Wall St. cocoon
He's painting the ceiling, the walls and the floor,

He's gonna lock himself up in his room
And when he emerges have a new change of style,
He keeps saying things like it's me and Howard Hughes
You'd wanna watch out for that dangerous smile.

'ME AND HOWARD HUGHES' EARLY DRAFT OF LYRICS

Ménage À Trois

The crowd went crazy 'doing the Rat'. In Ireland, in the UK, in the US. It became embarrassing. I mean the fucking thing was a joke, for God's sake!! It was also naff and outside Ireland had no context and made no sense whatsoever. Outside of Ireland, we thought it would lose us 'credibility' cos they weren't in on the in-joke and would imagine this is what we did. We would have become the very thing we were lampooning. Didn't matter – the punters loved it.

We also hated all the other local bands with their hideous jazz-funk 'fusion' bollox, their endless guitar/keyboard maunderings, the copyist funk or country outfits and the toe-gazing blues crowd.

They hated us too. One sad jazzer from the university pronounced, "The Boomtown Rats? Hopeless. They only know 3 chords." Correct. But what 3 chords! Having learned that the crowd we were building were also in on the joke, we branched out. And to be annoying and take the piss out of the musical snobs, I wrote a really crap, jazzy thing with LOTS of 7's and 9's (jazzy chords) about wanking – which is what I thought jazz was back then. A sort of musical wanking.

The song went on our 4-song demo which is what landed us our contract??? If I'd known the expression, then I would have used it ... I mean, WTF?

BOB GELDOF

Ménage À Trois

I've been reading your sex magazines
Take my ideas from the pictures I've seen
My mother didn't like them
She called them obscene
Said go wash your mouth with soap boy
Taste something clean

A ménage à trois
That's all I want to do in life
Ménage à trois
One and one and one is three
That's her and her and me
Seems alright!

Each night before sleep I'm a superman
Six girls in one night
It's easy with one hand

can't remember the rest...

Mind In Pocket

Say what you want

Stuffed air, muggy, thunderous July
Snatches of human drum 'n' bass rolling by
Noise intrudes into my interesting mood
Over half-read books
And half-eaten food
Upstairs they're staging the usual riot
But I'd prefer it to the silence
I'm more afraid of quiet
I need the cities shrieks
This night of urban charms
There's people on the street
Dancing to their car alarms

Put your mind in your pocket
Put your pocket
Where your mouth should be

Talk to a totally nude girl for a dollar
I'm in a topless mood
But my dick can't be bothered
I want to speak to a fully clothed person
For free I think
But I'm not really certain

BOB GELDOF

Monster Monkeys

Hey Mr. Mojo with your mop-top hair
And your eyes so greedy
With that half-lidded staring
At that hip-cocked lipstuck world
Where nobody cares
It's a long way down
But I can take you there

(don't you want me babe?)

Get out your laptop
Let's go Google map scrolling
Gonna get me some streetmap
Going downtown strolling
Gonna scratch hard
For an answer in vain
Written on the tattoos
On that overground train

(don't you want me babe?)

Black night in this part of town
You can bleed your nightmares
Put your arms around them
Better shake your moneymaker
Gotta pay your round
Shake that moneymaker
Til that last trumpet sounds

(don't you want me babe?)

Seven days I wandered
With a vomit on my soul
There was blood on the pillows
Cancer in my bones
There was lightning in my headspace
Darkness in my veins
There were monster monsoon monkeys
Sucking on my brain

(don't you want me babe?)

Mood Mambo

Somewhere up town late last night around 9 o'clock
There was a black snake crawling up the
Latin American stairs
With his
Slicked
Black
Cockroachair
He was greasy lightning
He was looking for someone else
He said "I know you, you know me, heyhey let's go see...
Y'know I'm in the Mood to Mambo..."
Yeah Bongo Crazy man.
Someone else pulled out a gun and said
"It's a little too late for that sort of thing...
If you think that you're the white/black snake don't go
messing with me...
I'm not in the mood"
Somebody else pulled,
I said "Don't be rude... just say Bongo Crazy maaan"
Yeh... bin there
Done that
Given every tit-for-tat
I'm for me
You're for you
Let's keep it that way
O.K??

Meanwhile
Later on underneath the river
Some frogman slipped
On his black beret
Over his skin
Tight rubbersuit.
Black boots
Looking for a place to go
An dive
Heading for the nearest divers skive
Looking for love

BOB GELDOF

On the cheap rate
Go!
Gonna make it down
with you wan
D'ja see?
He said
"Crazy bongo
I'm in the Mood to Mambo"

Meanwhile
We can watch the come
Dancing competitions
From the Midlands International Danceband Orchestra.
Lifting up their frilly chiffon skirts
They whirled and they twirled
In the late night rustle
To the beat of the muscle
Of the drum man
Inanin
Picking up the beat on the bongo skin
He was lookin for love underneath that din.
He was looking for me
He was looking for you
Till I walked up to the woman
And I said
(With a shoe)
I'm in the mooooood tooooo mambo
Bongo Crazy

Sssshhhh...
Let me into one of the secrets of this place
Y'see the late night
Flick knives
Glitter through the window
Careful where you go boy
Those knives are
Flick
Flack
Flagging through the dark, man
They're gonna cut

Your
Skin
I talked to Fr. Murphy and he swore he wouldn't tell
But some of those boys are gonna go to hell
See they're in the Mood to Mambo
Crazy Bongo
Cha cha cha
The fog horns scream
And the boys go "Woo Woo"
I don't mind
Cos I'm with you
We go bongo crazy
Yes we do
No we don't
Bongo crazy!!

BOB GELDOF

Dog Days they come
Is that saying anything
Buzzing around your head
Like unswatted flies
One day I'll get it together
+ Buy one of those electric blue fly killer thing
Mount it on the kitchen wall over there
+ Watch em fry (wouldn't yer)
Watch 'em die (couldn't us)
(Pass the time (shouldn't ye)
Pass the time ...... till ye

wouldn't ye

was creeping
Slow like the day

Baby Baby
Love falls away
Floats away
Melting in the April air
Summers coming
I caught it at the hill
Over-ripe already
Swill unfilled wouldn't you
Couldn't ye   Still unfilled   Couldn't ye
Unfulfilled   still unfilled   shouldn't you
Still unstill   + you did drink ye

'MUDSLIDE' EARLY DRAFT OF LYRICS

Hey Adrian I've been dreaming of deserts again
Crocodiles of weeping children press as slow as the sky
The
Crocodiles of weeping children pass as slow as the sky
Rain eyes the only source of water for
2,000 miles   What does it all mean
                   I woke up + sweat the night
                   everything's empty / so dusty
           - afraid   So arid
           - Dry   So dry
                    But you did

Hey adrian I've been dreaming of deserts again
Crocodiles of weeping children press as slow as the sky
Rain eyes the only source of water for 2,000 miles
What does it all mean?
I woke up + sweat the night
  everything's so dusty (wake up) So empty
                       (couldn't ya) So Arid (wouldn't ya)
                       (shouldn't ya) So Dry (couldn't ya)
  But you did didn't ya   + ya did didn't ya

BOB GELDOF

Mudslide

Dog days fall
Without saying anything
Razzing round your head
Like unwanted flies
One day I'll get it together
And buy one of those
Electric blue fly killer things
Mount it on the kitchen wall over there
And watch 'em fry (wouldn't you?)
Watch 'em die (couldn't you?)
Pass the time (shouldn't you?)
And you did... didn't you?

Baby, baby love falls away
Floats away
Melts into the April air
Summer's coming
I caught it on the hill
Over-ripe already
Still unfilled (wouldn't you?)
Unfulfilled (couldn't you?)
Still unstilled (shouldn't you?)
And didn't you?

Here we all are
Sitting on a mudslide
Are you on my side
Or are you on the other side's side
Here we all are
Standing in a minefield
How does your mind feel?
Standing in my field?

Hey Adrian, I've been dreaming of deserts again
Crocodiles of weeping children
Pass as slow as the sky
Their eyes the only source of water
For two thousand miles

BOB GELDOF

What does it all mean?
I wake up and I swat the night
But everything's so dusty
So empty
So arid (wouldn't you?)
So dry (couldn't you?)
But you did, didn't you?
Didn't you?

Here we all are
Sitting on a mudslide
Are you on my side
Or are you on the other side's side
Here we all are
Standing in a minefield
How does your mind feel?
Standing in my field?

I meant to say
I thought you knew
I always prayed
For me + you
The birthday suit
In which I was born
Is torn + frayed
ripped + worn
Nevermind

+ everything we've ~~been did~~ being
Has been undone
+ everything we didn't ~~been~~ did
~~half~~ Is left unsung
Has been + done
.. Nevermind

I meant to say
I thought you knew
I always prayed
For me + you.

My Birthday Suit

I meant to say
I thought you knew
I always prayed
For me and you
The birthday suit
In which I was born
Is torn and frayed
Is ripped and worn
Never mind

And everything we've been
Has been undone
And everything we did
Is been and gone
And left unsung

I meant to say
I thought you knew
I always prayed
For me and you
But never mind
It doesn't matter now

BOB GELDOF

My Blues Away

Don't wanna live
All by myself
The things I do
Affect my health
It make me deaf
It make me blind
Drive me half-crazy
Till I've almost lost my mind

Go check me out in the morning
Out in the day
Out in the evening
Won't you take
My blues away

This girl I knew
The things she'd do
The way she moved
The way she blew
She wanted my blood
Took me offa my feet
Opened up her oyster
And her pearl looked kinda neat

Don't check me out in the morning…

The way things are
They can't get worse
I've gotta go
Then I'll go first
If things get worse
Some say they must
They can't get better
'Cos my bubbles gonna burst

Don't check me out in the morning…

My Hippy Angel

All the birdies swimming in the sea
All the fishies hanging in the trees
All the people down on their knees
Rise up as one and sing

Love is all around
It's coming up from under the ground
Love like radiation
Radiate across the entire nation
Love for you and me
Moving out across the EEC
Love it goes so far
Travelling out across the USSR
Love going all the way
Stretching right across the USA
Love in Asia Minor
Africa, India, Australia and China
Come on

And in the middle of my troubled sleep
My hippy angel came to me
Saying chill out, be cool, stay free
I said I'm not sure what you mean
And she said

All the people in their cardboard boxes
The old and lonely in their tower blockses
The frightened ones who need some calm
My hippy angel said we all must chant
And all the birdies swimming in the sea
And all the people hanging from the trees
And all the fishies down on their knees
Rise up as one and sing
Love is all around.

She must be mad.

Neon Heart

Life pours down into the neon heart
Cement city is all a-sparks,
The morals are loose and the dames are all abroad,
There's a price on their heart you can't fail to afford,
Drink to the bitch and we'll dance for a while
If you can't do the nodule we'll love to try the glide,
It was all cool enough if you led the pays
The night was still young but it was all we had.

I picked her up at the bar that night,
I took her home she didn't put up a fight,
She was real good looking but she wasn't too bright
So I pulled the curtains and we locked out the night
I was fighting to maintain my cool,
I walked that thin line between animal and fool
Till I felt her hand in mine I said you're crazy about me,
I'm a boy from a good family —

The juke box was playing an out of time tune,
Made Trude cry Oh her mascara was ruined
She looked such a sight the sorrowful bitch,
She rushed to the bathroom and she slashed both her wrists
Everybody screamed and roared for more
Come stain angels shouting encore
Time was the enemy we had to kill it dead,
But the clock kept creeping round so I went to bed instead.

Neon Heart

Life pours down into the neon heart (It's late at night)
Cement City is all a-spark (Yeah, that's right)
The whores are loose and the dames are abroad (My pants are tight)
A price on their hearts you can't fail to afford.

Drink to the bitch and we'll dance for a while
If you can't do the Module than you'll have to try the Slide
It was all cool enough if you had the zazz
The night was still young and it was all we had

I picked her up at the bar that night (What did you do)
I took her home she didn't put up a fight (What did you do)
She was real good-lookin' but she wasn't too bright (So what's new)
We pulled the curtains and then locked out the night

I was fighting to maintain my cool
I walked the thin line between animal and fool
'Til I felt her hand in mine and said "You're wrong about me"
"I'm a boy from a good family" I told her

The juke box played an out-of-time tune (So what's new)
Made Tricia cry, oh her mascara was ruined (So what's new)
She looked such a sight, the sorrowful bitch (What did she do)
She rushed to the bathroom and she slashed both her wrists

Everybody screamed and roared for more
Lonestar angels shouting "Encore"
Time was the enemy, we had to kill it dead
The clock kept creeping round
So I went to bed instead.

BOB GELDOF

Never Bite The Hand That Feeds

Tell me what you're doing coming in so late at night
I wanna know
You say you're going out with childhood friends from way
   back when
Where do you go?
Tell us what you want, we'll give you anything
Just show respect for your daddy, little girl,
You know you never bite the hand that feeds.

Your mother's driven up the walls, you make too many calls
Who do you phone?
You use this place like some hotel, you want something you ring
   the bell
That's wrong
So tell us what you want, we'll give you anything
Just show some love for your mother, daughter dear
You know you never bite the hand that feeds

I don't know what went wrong
I couldn't understand
You grew up much too fast for me,
I wish it was before, like back when you were four
I had you on my knee and I told you lots of pretty things

Familial attention can't be bought like other toys, it can't be sold
And even if it could it wouldn't do you any good, you ought
   to know
I'll tell you what I want, I'll tell you what I need
I just need some money from my parents, father dear
And I'm going to bite your hand 'til it bleeds

With her friend Bill, and on the pill, she took a smallish flat
   in Sandycove
He wheels and deals, she cooks the meals and soon it ended up
   just like before
Way back at home
He tells her what he wants, he tells her what he needs
He says "just show respect for your man, little girl"
"You know you never bite the hand that feeds"

THE BOOMTOWN RATS, 1977

Never In A Million Years

I'd tear down the sky
Don't stop now
No never in a million years

I'd spit in their eye
Don't stop now
But I won't be a volunteer

And now
I'm always dreaming of dreams
That lie in state
Waiting for me to wake
And make
A life for them
I'll know I'll never let
Those self-defeating fears
Spoil those golden years
These days that pass us by
So slow

And now I
Always wander
Through fields that never stood
Can't see the trees through the wood
Or maybe – yes I could
Or no

I'll tear down the sky
Don't stop now
No never in a million years

BOB GELDOF

The New Routine

Sink with me beneath the waves
Drowning not waving
Stay a little
Dream a while
On loving and being loved

Brilliant shafts of chemical light
Pierce the gloom
Turn on the night
Talk to me a while
On loving and being loved

Whatja have to do to get a drink here
Whatja have to do to get a drink

Trip down to the great unconscious
Lose yourself feel slightly nauseous
Past nowhere, nothing
And the void between them
It's red and gold and orange too
This underwater's much too blue
Silent silver jellyfish sail pass you

The cushion's soft,
The fire's warm
The candle burns
This feels like home
I fall into your arms
Almost happy

It's not exactly Ovaltine
But welcome to the new routine

Whatja have to do to get a drink here

Nice 'N' Neat

Through tunnel vision watch him rant and rave
He says there's life beyond the grave
He wants his slice of the eternal cake
Well, God's in His Heaven and He's on the take.
That's nice and neat
It's bittersweet
But is it trick and treat
You're talking fast but
You're preaching feat

Bits and pieces I remember slightly
It was a long time ago
We'd have our hot and holy conversations
And solve the problems of a drunken world
Now a clerical collar chokes at your convictions
You strangle slowly for the old addiction
It's Heaven's army and you're so professional
But listen closely to this closed confessional.

We'd take a recipe for religion
And bring it to the theological kitchen
Mix it up to make your own concoction
Believed in God but you'd shake a fist at him

And Ray isn't that holy
Hey Ray isn't that hard?
Ah Ray it isn't that easy
Now

You said you spoke to God and asked a question
You were wondering "what's the use of it all?"
He said everybody does what they want to
Provided that it's true, that's all

You said, hey Big G there's my problem
I'm not so sure 'bout what's true
He said I'll let you in on my big secret Ray
The final truth is –
There is no truth!
And
Na-na-na-na, bop shoo wop shoo wop

BOB GELDOF

Night Turns To Day

Baby in the dead of the night
When my head's going round
It's burning, burning
Things that fill the heart with dread are messing up my head
I'm tossing, turning
Eyes that bore a hole through x-ray proof walls
Staring through the pit of my soul
Once I saw an insane man break his teeth
Trying to chew through iron bars

In the dark of 2am when I see you there
Breathing easy
Breathe that angel's breath on me
Breathe away the fears
So I sleep peacefully

Innocence will always be
The one true moral alibi
But I should never try to protect you
From growing up aware of our crimes

And when
The night turns to day
Dark turns to grey
And leaves me
Tired and lonely
Night turns to day
And dark turns to grey
And leaves me
alone with those memories now

Must it always be
That we of necessity
Acquire understanding
And with that knowledge must we gain
All the mental pain
Of comprehension

The man stood only inches from my face
Intelligence sparked in his eyes
His gums a mute and bleeding mess of teeth
The people who were with me laughed till they cried

Night turns to day and finds me
Tired and cold again
Night turns to day
And finds me alone with these memories
Night turns to day
And blows away all of those stories

I never think that there's any of this will touch you
But baby your mummy and daddy are praying
That this world we leave will turn out good for you

BOB GELDOF

No Hiding Place

You'd like to be something
But you don't know what
Why are you hiding your head
like some human Angkor Wat

Then you fall down on your knees
And you begin to pray
But spiritually speaking
You're an easy lay
That's what they say

Sooner or later
You'll get yours kid
I don't know when
But I hope for your sake it's quick

Don't turn your head away from the searchlight glare
Like a rabbit in the headlights
But you can't be sick or scared
When there's no hiding place

Well I've seen you naked and I prefer you dressed
And I've seen you without make-up
And I wasn't impressed
So what? So nothing, don't be upset
It's not what you got, it's what you gonna get

So take a lesson from me that can't be learned
It's not what you spend, it's what you've earned
Does your stomach feel small, do your sinus ache
You're trying to dream when you should be wide awake

When there's no hiding place

No Small Wonder

I got home last night about 8
There was nothing on the T.V. as usual
Just the normal repeats and things
I had the City Prices edition of the Evening Standard
Which was not as good as the Late Night One
Mainly because it doesn't have the full cinema listings
To be more specific it doesn't have the Fulham ABC
Which is my local
So I walked over to Battersea Park
Down by the Sri Chimnoy Mile
Past the Peace Pagoda
It's good
You can have a personal religious experience
And get healthy at the same time
Which obviously is important for a busy man like me
Well another moment in life's great adventure
It's no small wonder

I hope you weren't offended by what happened last night
It was the awkward hour
And I didn't know what to do
Whether to come on or just leave it
To be honest I wasn't that interested
And I didn't think you were either
So I went back to my place
And you went back to yours
And I got into bed
And started reading a book
By a guy called Tobias Woolf
It's good it's short stories
Just before you sleep he'll take
You off to Burma... Mandalay
Places like that
I set the alarm clock ready for another day at work
Another day in life's great adventure
It's no small wonder

BOB GELDOF

No Tomorrow Like Today

You keep saying diamond rings don't do it for you
Babe there's more rocks on your knuckles
That are bigger than an Oppenheim mine
And now it's late in the P.M.
You'd got to carpe that diem
You're way out of line
And way out of time
You'd better seize that day

Cos there's no tomorrow quite like today
There's no tomorrow
You could beg steal or borrow
You're throwing your dice
Your I Ching and Tarot
But they all agree
There's no tomorrow like today

I don't want to break when I shake you
I'm just trying to wake you up girl
They might put me on a charge
But I'd get off for justifiable cause
Cos no jury would convict me
Saying "yea he's strictly guilty
But unanimously we all agree
We got one thing to say"

There's no tomorrow like today...

Sometime honey it feels like
It's a Shakespeare play that we're in
If he had to do a re-write
You'd be a Hamlet in skirts
Oh my little procrastinator
You delayer and prevaricator
I prognosticate
I ain't gonna wait
Or hang any longer

246   B-SIDE OF 'TRASH GLAM BABY', 2020

Cos there's no tomorow like today...

There's a whole world waiting out there for us two
But what it is we're meant to do
I haven't got a hunch or clue
But it involves me and you
You need to take the longer view

There's no tomorrow like today

BOB GELDOF

Nothing Happened Today

Turn on the TV
Turn on the radio.
Turn down that sound
Turn down that sound

Open the curtains
Open the windows.
What's happening around
What's happening around

I'll do some washing
I might go shopping
I'm going downtown
I'm going downtown

Someone told me, "nothing happened today".

I woke up late
I had a headache
I went back to sleep

I stood there waiting
Waiting for something
There wasn't a thing
Not even one thing

Someone told me, "nothing happened today".

Harry Hooper living in No. 10
Bought a toupée and glued it to his head
"It looks very natural," everybody said.
But then his wife said, "Toupée, isn't that a French word?"
And Harry said, "Olé." She said, "That's a Spanish verb"
And he said, "O.K., can't tell the difference these days."

I watched ITV
Cos I wanted to see
The late news at 10
It came on and then

She shuffled her papers
She swivelled in her chair
She looked up and said

The weather was fair
And then it turned cold
It started to rain
Pouring with rain.

Some people died
Some people were born
And some stayed the same
And some went insane

Tomorrow's Wednesday
Today was Tuesday
And this is the date
March 28th

It was the morning
Then afternoon
And then the night came
And then the night came

Oh… and someone told me, "Nothing happened today."
Yes, someone told me, "Nothing happened today."
It happened today.

BOB GELDOF

One For Me

You're a lotta laughs, ain't you, babe.
You cracked me up I laughed so much I nearly died.
It's so funny I was weeping.
Cried so hard. I nearly split my side.

I watched you laughing on the T.V.
I don't get it said the kindly host.
But there are many here among us
Who feel the sight is but a joke.

Your imagination's running riot.
Sometimes I swear you believe what you say.
No-one seems to notice it's the same joke.
It's just told in a thousand different ways.

And I can't wait to read the new ones.
Yeah the comedy just gets better every day.
You're a lotta laughs ain't you baby.
It's funny how it all turned out that way.

You should have known better.
It's not for you.
This one's for me.

I saw a picture of you grinning.
Yeah that smirk covered your entire face.
It almost split your head in two.
I hear you sold it to OK.

Sell a photo of you laughing.
The more you hoot the more they pay.
You don't even need to get your clothes off anymore.
You're a bit too old for that stuff anyway.

Somebody saw you at the party.
You did the one where you're falling flat on your face.
You had the whole place cracking up in stitches.
Apparently you fall with such good grace.

SEX, AGE & DEATH, 2001

And the teenage clothes and see-through sizes.
The mutton dished up on the Sunday plate
Is now the lamb in Ghostly guises.
It's all done in the best of taste.

You should have known better.
It's not for you.
This one's for me.

BOB GELDOF

One Of The Girls

When I was a young man
Barely 16
You were my pretty thing
In pink shirt, blue jeans
You always told me
You wanted the world
You could have never been
Just one of the girls

Now I'm a grown man
The years passed us by
I still remember
Sometimes I cry
I hear about you
Still wild and still free
You wanted the world
Once the world was me

Don't look
Stay away
If you see me
I'll walk away

One hundred flowers
For love that's alive
One pressed and dried
For love that died

BOB GELDOF

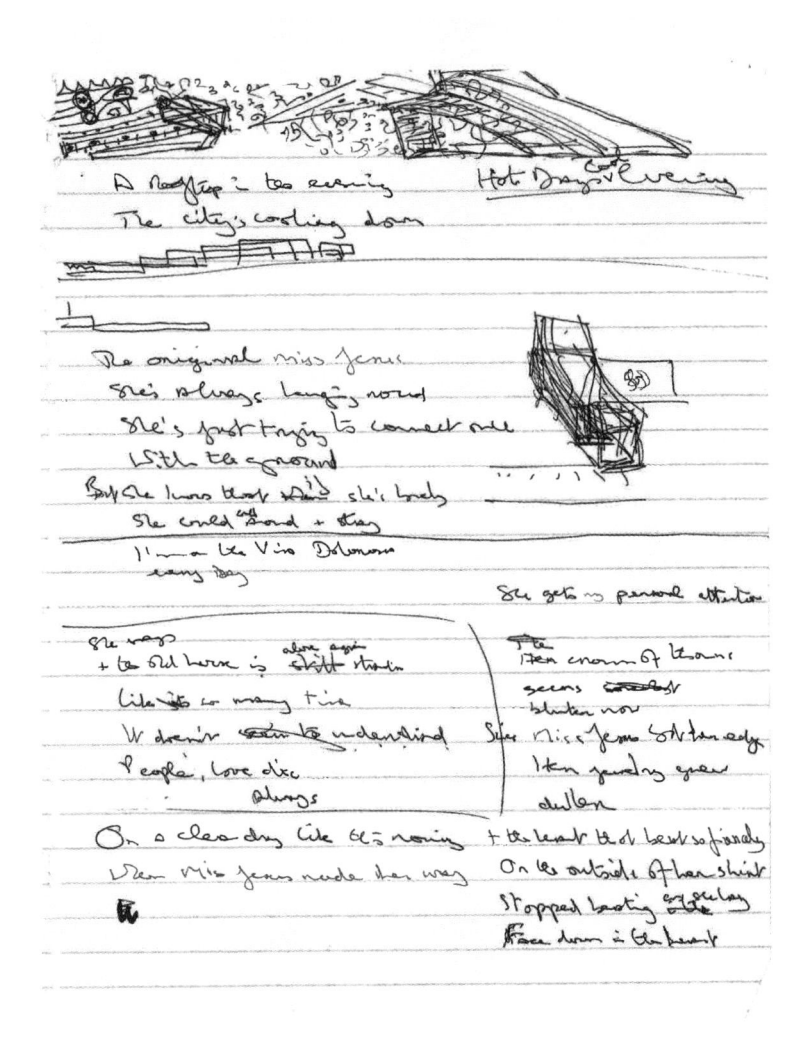

'THE ORIGINAL MISS JESUS' DRAFT OF LYRICS

BOB GELDOF

The Original Miss Jesus

The original Miss Jesus
Yea she's always hanging 'round
She's just waiting to connect once
With the ground

And she knows that if she's lonely
She can come around and stay
I'm on the Via Dolorosa
Every day

The old house is alone
Like so many times
It doesn't understand
Love and people always die

And the heart that beat so fiercely
On the outside of her shirt
Stopped beating as she lay down
In the dirt

Her crown of thorns seem blunter
Since Miss Jesus lost her edge
Now her jewellery just grows duller
On the ledge

The original Miss Jesus
Yea she's always hanging 'round
Hanging 'round

Out Of Order

I got a brand-new car
And I went snarling
Up 'round Oxford St.,
Policeman stopped me
And said "no private cars
Allowed on my beat"
So baby quick
Abandon ship
Jumped a bus that took me to the bridge
All the way to Brixton Fridge

The Fridge was freezing
And I began to feel much worse
The river flowed
But the banks looked they were going to burst
So feeling weird I quickly grew a beard
And thought "nobody's gonna notice you"

You're out of order
Yea you are
Like breaking down
You're out of order
Yes you are
You don't work now

Well I'm not sure about tomorrow
But yesterday
They told me
Live for today
And the rest will follow

And now I'm laughing
I know cos I can hear that noise
Nobody moves
But I know I'm dancing
With the other party boys

BOB GELDOF

Cos when you lose the plot
Like I tend to do
They're gonna hang a sign on you
Saying

Out of order
You're breaking down
You're out of order
You don't work now
So, won't you come around?

Ah look at you now,
You look good,
you're all lit up tonight,
+ don't be afraid
No, don't be scared, you'll be alright
~~This is all give you the~~
Throw me a line
give me a smile
Help in it out for you
We're better than this
You know that's true

BOB GELDOF

Over Again

Well look at you now
Don't you look good
You're all lit up tonight
Don't be afraid
No, don't be so scared
We'll make it our world tonight

And I felt a kiss ring out
When peace broke out last night, yeah
I felt that shot across my bow
Going over and over and over again
Shot down like before
And over and over and over again
Another blank that scores
But I wouldn't mind
I'll sleep in a little while now now
Yes I'll stay awake
And I'll sleep with you

Throw me a line give me a smile
'n I'll spin it out for you
We're better than this
You know that's true
Love; and the world spits at you

But I felt a kiss ring out
When peace broke out last night, yeah
I felt that shot across my bow
Going over and over and over again
Shot down like before and
Over and over and over again
Another blank that scores
But I'll stay awake
I'll sleep a little while now now
I'll stay awake
And I'll sleep with you

Going over and over and over again
Shot you down like before and
And over and over and over again
Another blank that scored
And over and over and over again
All sweet light and reason
Over and over and over again
Through these desperate seasons

No, I wouldn't mind
I'll sleep in a little while now now now now
Yes I'll stay awake
And I'll sleep with youv

BOB GELDOF

Pale White Girls

Pale white girls.
Look for love.
Pale white bodies.
Stretch for love.

Scratching the flesh.
Scraping of bones.
Limbs that are trembling babe.
For something to hold.

Languid and liquid.
Well maybe I'll stay.
Marbled and ghostly girls.
Take me away.

Your mouth on my body.
In this tall room.
Crushed, bruised and crimson.
Lit by the moon.
The fluorescent moon.

Sacred those hours.
Away from the storm.
Wrenched from the deepest pits.
Crying 'Reborn, Reborn, Reborn'.

And I will not follow.
And I will not lead.
Your permissions to bleed.
Have been guaranteed.
By the one.
Whose approval you seek.

Pale white girls.
Scratch for love.
Pale white bodies.
Stretch for love.

The crucifix stares.
From its hip-cocked heights.
But I hold the secrets now.
Velvet the night.
Velvet the night.

And I will not follow.
Why waste my time.
My permission to bleed.
Has been guaranteed.
By the one.
Whose approval I need.

BOB GELDOF

Passing Through

Today in the park
I thought I saw you
That afternoon light
Plays those tricks on you
Why didn't you tell me
You were only passing through
You passed through me
As you were passing through
Didn't you

We will not break
We will not bend
We'll take these rented souls
And render them
Immune to loss or pain
We'll just pretend
It's all the same

Today in the café
I thought I saw you
Smoke filters through the window
Playing those tricks on you
Why didn't you tell me
You were only passing through
Stopping here a little while
While you passing through
Didn't you

We'll just pretend
That nothing's changed

Pity The Poor Drifter

It was late and it was Tuesday
And the wind rattled down the street
And I caught my face in every man
Who looked worn and tired and beaten

It is wisdom she said that has killed you
I know less but I understand more
And no rain nor snow nor sleet nor ice
Could have chilled me more to the core

Many years have passed since then
I haven't lived but I've got by
I wrote back once
No reply

Go down, go down, go down in your slow sky
Sink low you traitorous sun
Denied by Life
Denied by Love
Then my time here has been done

BOB GELDOF

Please Don't Go

I was walking down the street
I was walking down the street with the Queen of Hearts.
She does the Monkey, the Polish and the Spit,
I do the all-age favourite the epileptic fit.
Polo-neck, polo-neck, she don't wear a shirt
I suppose it's because it disguises the dirt.
Hey, where you going with that hat on your head?
"Down to the graveyard to visit the dead."
Please don't go
A worm in one ear and a slug in the other,
It doesn't look like her, are you sure that it's mother?
Please don't go... now please.

Pulled Apart By Horses

If I stand up on the wall again
And looking round I see the mote in every eye
And the sky chokes up with dust
That spirals into black infinity and things
And I feel your heat
I feel it all around
Then take my hand
Fade into light
I feel the strain
And you say alright
These things will pass
Nothing can last
At least not like this I think

But how does it feel?
Pulled apart by horses that's how I feel

If I called out all the places where
Brutality still stamps and tramples everything
And the dignity of peoples lives
Lives only in their eyes and in their suffering
For the third and second rate ideas
Whose time has been and gone
Then take my hand
Straighten me out
You say o.k.
But be in no doubt
These things exist because of our love
Of cheap ideology

So how does that feel
Pulled apart by horses that's how I feel

BOB GELDOF

Put Out The Cat

Bring in the dog
Put out the cat
Leave on your boots
Your pearls and hat
Yea break out the drugs man
Cos that's where I'm at
And break me down
Then put me back
On track
I go

Ooo shalalala
This love ain't easy
Ooo sha lalala
Nothing's easy
Oooshalalala
Our love ain't easy
Ooshalalala
Who said it was easy

I don't know what
But something's cracked
So please excuse my lack of tact
I'll put out the dog
So bring out your cat

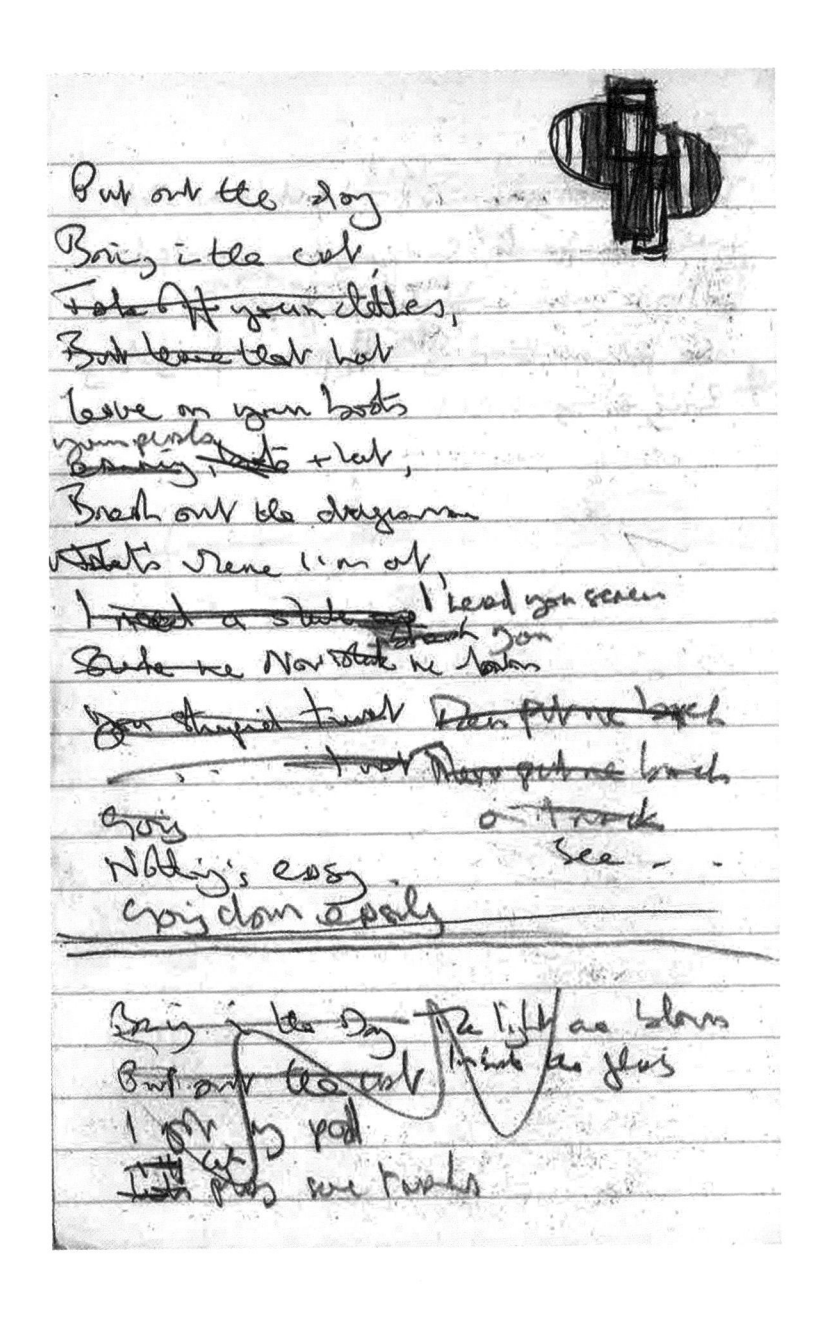

'PUT OUT THE CAT' EARLY DRAFT OF LYRICS

Rat Trap

The abattoir was a sort of bovine death camp. Those who worked there as indifferent to the killing as any order-obeying Gulag guard. You did your job in as efficient a manner as possible amidst the clanking of hooks and chains and clanging sluices, swinging carcasses, hissing pneumatic killing bolts, busy-buzzing butcher saws, automated flaying knives, steam belching bone macerators, gutters of rushing bloodied water and the ever present swish of pressure hoses spraying the offal and shit-strewn walls and floors. And of course the bellowing of tight-packed, panicked animals who hours before had been aimlessly mulching the rich, rain-soaked grass of Ireland and who were now being forced in single line onto the sloping, aluminium gunnel that was barely the width of their body, their feet unable to grip or take purchase on the curving metal floor and a blank steel door in front of them.

They could not turn, nor could they go back – though many tried. They were confused, frightened and sniffing at what lay behind the door through which they could hear their fellows bellow, followed by a terrifying silence save for the mechanical racket of the killing floor.

Abruptly, the door swung sideways, the cow fell through, a quick glimpse of chains and hooks and then a human put a metal gun to its forehead. A long hose connected the gun to an air cylinder, the trigger was pulled, an explosive pump of air plunged the retractable bolt into the animal's brain and withdrew in an angry hiss. It crumpled, instantly dead, chains whipped immediately around the hind legs, back legs broken, the carcass rapidly hauled into the air, knives slashed its throat, blood poured into waiting vats (later to be delicious black pudding) and perhaps no more than five minutes later – hoopla!! Steak, ribs, haunch, bone meal. By which time there were another four or five carcasses swinging immediately behind it.

6am. Breakfast at the Meat Factory...

Paul and I worked there. I called him Billy in the song 'Rat Trap'. It scanned better. I didn't like him. I was afraid of him. Small, little rat-face. Wiry, twitchy and very violent. He carried an axe in the waistband of his trousers. He'd wink at me as if the two of us were in on some huge conspiratorial joke together, and tap the axe hidden under the white butcher coats we all had to wear. 'Fuggin' 6 stitcher a' deh wheeghen Robert' grinning malevolently. The success or otherwise of any weekend was determined by how much sickening hurt he could inflict on whomever. He could invite or incite the violence, or simply randomly attack anyone he felt like. Didn't matter really. In the pub, on the street wherever. He was a psychopath. 'A 6 stitcher' of course meant someone's head had been smashed open by this little shit and been duly sewn up. If they were lucky.

I don't know why he decided this middle-class Southside kid – me, should be the father confessor to his ugliness. If he was trying to shock and frighten me it worked but he seemed oblivious to that. I don't think he was trying to impress me either because I would ask why he did those things. I didn't ask in a hand-wringing, whingey, whiny upset middle classy way, nor with a priest's soft, faux understanding of the confessional-type voice. He just pissed me off and yet he kept hanging round me. Much to my discomfort.

He had a girlfriend. Judy. Much more on the case than him. They lived in the 5 Lamps part of town. Not safe for me. He took me there once or twice. There wasn't really an option whether to go or not. He just said we were going and would look me directly and meaningfully in the face. He was much smaller than me and his little rat-face would peer up, eyes slanted to almost closed and a little rictus smile on his mouth. 'Yea sure Paul.' I was never there when he attacked someone.

The pub he drank in reeked of always-on violence. Hard men sound admiring. I didn't admire them. Sometimes Judy would ask him when he was going to do, 'something proper'. It was embarrassing going out with someone who worked in a slaughterhouse. 'Y'always fuggin' stink. Like a fuggin' farmer' (the worst insult). He mumbled and was surprisingly compliant around her… oh well.

It was hopeless. He was hopeless. There wasn't a hope in hell for him or all the others. And the truth is although I knew I was only there to get enough to 'move on' – to what or where I didn't know but I knew I was moving on – Dublin wasn't it. And if I stayed much longer, I could be Paul.

I wrote 'Rat Trap' in the slaughterhouse. I didn't know I was writing a song. It started off as a short story. Became a 'poem' and when we needed one last song for our second album it became that track. It became our first number one and the first rock 'n roll Irish number one. Ever. I suppose every British kid felt the same hopelessness that was on offer in 1978.

But Billy (Paul), like Joey in the earlier song, were Dublin and then finally there was Frank.

Knew him well. Good guy. Civil service office job. The holy fucking grail. Hard to come by. Everybody wanted one. Cos you were safe. If you couldn't be a priest or a farmer – job for life and a 'dacent pinshin' – then the Civil Service was yer man. Set you up for the long haul. He hated it but he too, like the guys above, was stuck. He was afraid and so bored of the utter drudgery of the deskbound blank fluorescent nothingness that became his life. Part of me envied his salary but only to a very small point. Got grief from the wife for his lack of ambition. Drudgery at work, bitterness at home. Stuck. The four of us. Joey, Billy, Frank and Me.

I got out. I became a rock star. No pension, but the fine drugs and beautiful women compensated... and anyway we were going to be young forever weren't we?

There are a thousand other stories I could tell you about so many of the songs but then there are TOO many songs and I don't have the time and neither do you.

We left Dublin.

'You are now
In London, that great sea, whose ebb and flow at once is deaf and loud,
And on the shore vomits its wrecks, and still howls on for more.
Yet in its depths what treasures! You will see...'
Percy Bysshe Shelley

That was us. Vomited on the shores of that great city and we were deaf and loud and howling for more, and we dove deep, deep down and unlike so many others we DID find its wondrous treasures.

But all those are for '*More* Tales of Boomtown Glory' and best kept for now for another day ...

Rat Trap

There was a lot of rocking going on that night,
Cruising time for the young bright lights,
Just down past the gasworks, by the meat factory door,
The Five Lamps Boys were coming on strong,
The Saturday night city beat had already started
The pulse of the corner boys sprang into action
And young Billy watched it under the yellow street light
And said "tonight, of all nights, there's gonna be a fight"

He doesn't like it living here in this town
He says the traps have been sprung
Long before he was born
He says hope bites the dust behind all the closed doors
And pus and grime ooze from its scab-crusted sores
There's screaming and crying in the high rise blocks
It's a rat-trap Billy but you're already caught
But you can make it
If you want to
Or you need it bad enough
You're young and good-looking
And you're acting kind of tough
Anyway it's Saturday night time to see what's going down.
Put on the bright suit Billy head for the right side of town
It's only 8 o'clock but you're already bored
You don't know what it is but there's got to be more
You'd better find a way out,
Hey kick down the door
It's a rat-trap and you've been caught

In this town Billy says "everybody
Tries to tell you what to do"
In this town Billy says "everybody
Says you gotta follow rules"
You walk up to those traffic lights
Switch from your left to your right
You push in that button,
And when that button comes alight
It tells you

"Walk don't walk,
Talk don't talk"
Hey Billy take a walk... with me.

Little Judy's trying to watch Top of the Pops
But mum and dad are fighting don't they ever stop,
She takes down her coat and walks out on the street,
It's cold on that road, but it's got that home beat,
Deep down in her pocket she finds 50p
Now is that any way for a young girl to be,
"I'm gonna get out of school work in some factory,
Work all the hours God gave me
Get myself a little easy money"

Her mind's made up, she walks down the road,
Her hands in her pockets, coat buttoned 'gainst the cold,
She finally finds Billy down at the Italian café
And when he's drunk it's hard to
Understand what Billy says
But then he mumbles in his coffee and he suddenly roars,
"It's a rat-trap and we've been caught..."

Ratified

Take me back to Boomtown
I'll be ratified
Circumscribed
And ratified and blue

Take me back to Boomtown
And I'll be ossified
Face down in the gutter
With no shoes

BOB GELDOF

Ratlife

I've been living all my life
In a Ratlife
I can't take it anymore

I've been living off the floor
In a Ratlife
It gets you down

And now my autumn leaves are burning
That turning trick from red to gold
And I can feel my winters coming
Blowing cold

Real Different

The world at any time
Might take it's own thalidomide
It's just one of those things

You see eternity fell out of luck
When we invented self destruct,
It's just one of those things

But now you're walking in, you're walking out
You're stepping in and stepping out
Cos who an' who is kidding you
With mystery clues to points of view
That never meant a thing

Let's get drunk tonight and watch the T.V.
It's much too dark tonight
I'll fill my pockets full of stones
And throw them at the light
Cos I stop and I think,
Well it could be different
A new day
But it's different
It's all changed
But it's no different
So stop and walk away

I don't want to argue with you
Anyway the end results always the same
It's just that tuned into the never-never
Everything will seem forever
Ain't it always the same?
Their beaming local hope out on the stereo waves
Salvation's on the dial but a foot's in the grave
So you stop and you think
Well it's real different
It's not new
But it seems different
It's all changed

BOB GELDOF

But it's no different
Stop and turn away
For more of the same

It's those little things they do
That scare me so
Something in their smile
That tells me things ain't kosher

And I want to be different,
And I want to be dangerous
Doctor what's the cure?
Tonight another ceremony
Tonight is not like other nights
I'm almost sure
The doctor clicks his tongue
At this real head case
Who's just a wicker chair away
From re-habilitation
He stops and he thinks
This could be different
A new day
But it's no different
It's all changed
But it's no different

Roads Of Germany

I'm driving on the road Hitler built
I'm driving on the road that Hitler built
This is the place where history stopped to shit
And I'm driving on the road Hitler built

I'm driving on the road that Stalin built next
There's more holes in Joe's than Adolf's
But what would you expect
And I wonder what the Germans did
To fall from history's nest
I'm driving on the road that Stalin built next

On the roads of Germany
On the roads of Germany
These are the roads of the 20th Century
And there's blood and steel and leather
Mixed into that concrete
When you're riding on the roads of high Germany

I'm cruising on Konrad's Autobahn
Konrad's got a Beetle and Ludwig a Trabant
And Willy's got a Merc and Erich's got a tank
But that road only took me to a concrete dead end trap

We're driving on the road that never ends
All roads lead to exit signs and then they start again
And Helmut's building on the wheel of history as it spins
And history never ends 'cos it's too busy beginning

On the roads of Germany
On the roads of Germany
These are the roads of the 20th Century
And there's blood and steel and leather
Mixed into that concrete
When you're riding on the roads of high Germany

And I'm walking in a Black Forest lane
And I step into the trees for to get some leafy shade

BOB GELDOF

And I fall asleep in some dappled sunlit glade
And I dream and in my dream I am lost and afraid
And it grows dark,
It grows damp and I shiver and I'm cold
And deep inside the forest something obscenely old
Stirs and shakes and comes awake and in its putrid pit
It belches and it squirms in its own dirt and filth
And slithers on its stinking slime while everything
    holds its breath
And its slow thighs, blank eyes pitiless as the past
Reborn from its fitful sleep, its hour come again at last
Slouches towards its own Jerusalem to be re-cast
And in my horror I recognise myself in it as it passes
Familiar and repulsive and as old as mortal man
This philosophy of brutality, ignorance and hate
Buried deep in everyone waiting to escape
And you must kill it before it kills you and everything in its wake
And I take my knife and I kill it, and it screams and then I wake
And I'm terrified and horrified and in this mortal state
I stagger toward the curbside of the 4 lane motorway
"Drive" I say and we drive and soon I stop shaking
But I can't stop thinking
'bout these dreams and revelations
Except its not a dream its real and its of our own making
And it's not just Germany its everywhere and the
whole world is a-quaking
As we turn onto this road we all seem to be taking
And you can't help thinking these things on the
roads of Germany

THE HAPPY CLUB, 1992

Rock 'n Roll YéYé

Yea yea rock 'n roll
You always did it for me
C'mon, c'mon rock 'n roll
Still doing it for me

Six o'clock another morning
Working like a dog each day
Light creeps underneath the awning
Slaps my sleeping face awake
Your breath it fills me like this morning
Your body fills me with the night
And Monday hears the weekend calling
Break out babe
Let's hit the red lights
All night
Alright
Singing

Coats still hanging in the hallway
Empty of their human shape
The bodies that once filled them
Left behind a hole in space
See it gets so hard to stay alive sometime
Some days you can barely face
But it's not just you that gets so lonely
I'm told it's everybody
In the human race
They're outta place
In outer space
Singing

BOB GELDOF

Room 19

1989 prefaced our time. Three events occurred which were the trumpet blast of the Now. That old post-war system which had frozen the world in stasis finally collapsed. A young British scientist in Switzerland wrote code that he called The World Wide Web and Deng Xiaoping of China applied for membership of the WTO. Hello, you 21st century schizoid men (as King Crimson correctly prophesied).

I travelled through that time. I think I felt it coming. It's odd to travel on the autobahn of Germany if you are of my vintage. These were the wide roads built by the Nazi gangsters that would enable the easy transportation of tanks etc. which facilitated the speedy invasion of other countries. And here you are cruising smoothly along until you get to the bumpy bit. The bit that hasn't been repaired since 1945. And then as it wakes you from the troubled dreams that accompanied sleep on those roads, you dimly realise, "Oh fuck ... we're in the East." Commie roads. It made me think. And it made me think that something's happening and it's neither good nor bad, it's just a bit different and it all continues. It was not "the end of history" as has been written, rather "History never ends/Cos it's too busy beginning" ('The Roads Of Germany').

Then everything went pear-shaped Soviet-wise and man, the weird stuff they found and found out amongst the wreckage of the re-birth of an older Russia was bonkers really. One was an unnoticed and forgotten room deep in the bowels of the vast Kremlin palace. Room 19 (so Orwell!!) had shelves where the brains of the great Soviet geniuses (and there were many) were preserved in formaldehyde inside big glass jars. 'Geniuses' like Lenin and Stalin etc. and actual non-murderous tyrannical nutters like glorious Pasternak and brave, brilliant Sakharov and a host of others. The plan, apparently, was to discover precisely how and why these people excelled in their chosen field. In Stalin's case mass murder, in Pasternak's literature. Was there a common physical thread? (No.) Was there something that somehow could be discerned or determined as to why there was exceptionalism present? (Again ... no.) Scientists were instructed to thinly slice the gooey messes and examine closely for traces of difference to the ordinary. There wasn't any, but I bet the poor fuckers who had to slice up Uncle Joe's foetid little mind-sack reported immediate success for fear of being dispatched forthwith to the furthest Gulag of that infinite archipelago of despair. They were all mad.

But it was funny. I thought so anyway. So ... (bear with me now) I thought what would happen if say, I was gigging in Moscow, had a heart attack, died, and recognising my undisputed genius they stashed my brain alongside all the other lads up there on their shelves? Obviously, the only way preserved brains can communicate is through mind telepathy ... (still with me?) Well, it stands to reason that everyone would want to know who the new boy was (i.e. Me) and would begin chatting mind-to-mind as it were. But equally obviously there would be non-stop rows and arguments between the political and scientific and literate types. The noise was appalling and I just wanted to get out. See where I'm coming from ...? "When I was dead I thought I'd be free" 'Room 19'.

That was then. Nobody will get it now I suppose.

'ROOM 19' DRAFT OF LYRICS

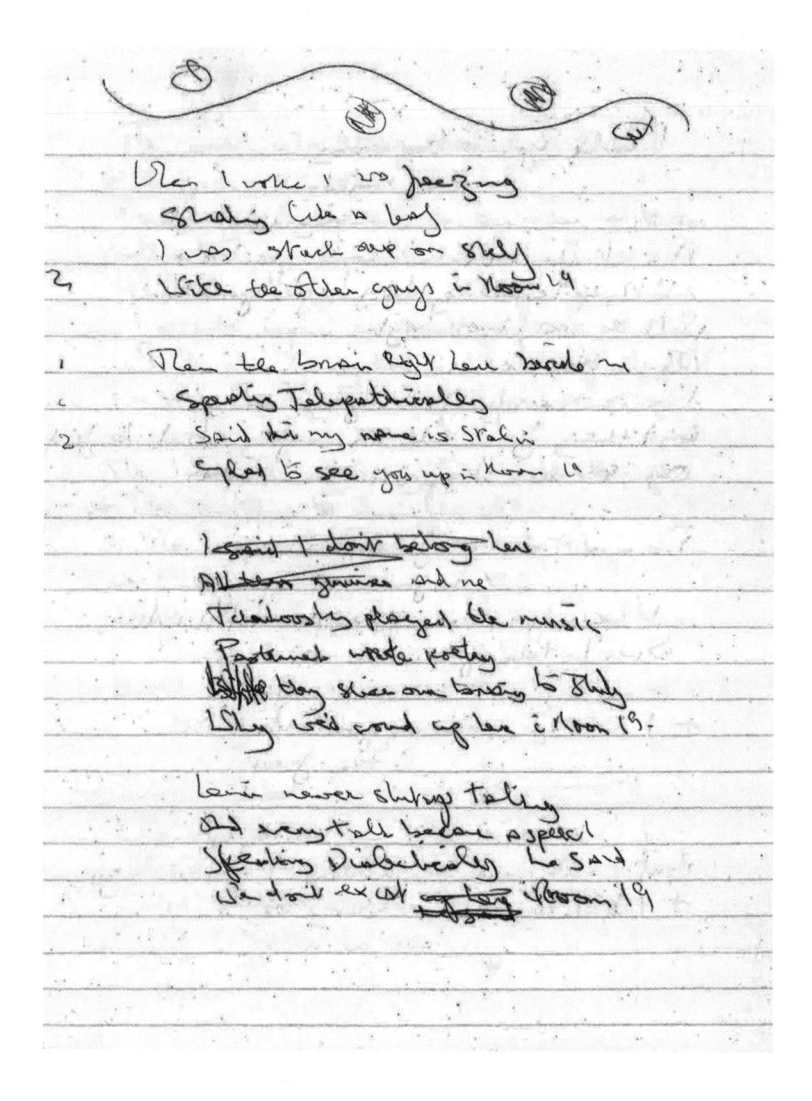

BOB GELDOF

Room 19 (Sha La La La Lee)

Sha-la-la-la-la
Sha-la-la-la-lee
Sha-la-la-la-la
I feel free

When I woke up I was freezing
Shaking like a leaf
I was stuck up on a shelf
With the other guys in Room 19

Then the brain here right beside me
Speaking telepathically
Said "Hi, my name is Stalin
Glad to see you here in Room 19"

Yeah Tchaikovsky played the music
While Pasternak wrote poetry
As they sliced our brains to study
Why we ended up in Room 19

Lenin never shut up talking
And every talk became a speech
"Speaking dialectically" He said
"We don't exist in Room 19"

Well 'ol Sakharov was outraged
And said "Exactly what you mean?"
And Lenin said "There is no heaven
So I can't believe in Room 19"

When I was dead
I thought I'd be free

BOB GELDOF

Say Hi To Mick

Say hi to Mick for me
Tune him out through Channel KGB
I always thought that I would be
In New York City when I grew old
In New York City when I grew cold

It's cold out here
And this is home
And you know there's snow everywhere I go
But it don't look like any place I know

The son of the Soviet ambassador was sent back to Moscow. As he left he said "Say hi to Mick Jagger".

Scream In Vain

Money in my pocket down at
Scream In Vain
Come on
Lambs led to the slaughter
They cut you in second down at
Scream In Vain
Come on
Lambs led to the slaughter

Sweet Yams in the fields of Harbo
Made me feel better
They took the straw from off the roof
To make the fire catch as it should
They boil the water and they cook the roots
For them it's new
For me old fruits
But more precious now than it's ever been
We share the food in the noonday heat
Sweet Yams in the fields of Harbo
The mountains roll
Green on green
The mountains roll
Green on green

BOB GELDOF

She Said NO.

Late last night she called me on the telephone
Late last night I was watching telly on my own
She "we need to talk"
I put her on the speakerphone and let squawk
Sat back and watched Man U.
2-1 at home and
I said "I love you so"
just then Man City score another goal
I thought football's just like love
But she said NO!

She said we needed to talk of our relationship
She said she wasn't happy and that I was too insensitive
She said "where d'you think we're going?"
I said "search me Honeybun, how would I know
But do you want a Biriani to go"
She said NO!
She said "you're messed up in the head"
I said "the answer to our problems lies between my legs"
I don't think she got the joke when she screamed
NO!

Well I'm her Long Tall Daddy and she's my gonest girl
We're the coolest cats but we're occupying different worlds
It's as incompatible as that
It like she's Officer Dibble and I'm Top Cat
But I guess that's how we roll when she says
No
She says "you're such a selfish pig"
I say "fair enough baby" trying to be sensitive
You should watch that volcano blow
When she says NO!

Arrrggghhh!!!! you fuckin' PRICK!!!!!!
NO!!

She's A Lover

She's a lover and she fits inside my head
She's a lover but there's nothing happening in my bed
She's a lover but she won't be back
She's a lover and I got the sack
I can't take it
Or take her back

It's been raining and I've been sitting here all afternoon
It started snowing so I turned the light on in my room
She's a lover but the loving's gone
She's a lover she's a smoking gun
Bang, bang
You're done

Now I'm a man with all this
Weird stuff inside his head

I loved her like the early leaves of spring
That weigh the branches of those waking trees
The best of us is Love she'd say
The rest of us dust and decay
Then my love turned away

BOB GELDOF

(She's Gonna) Do You In

Watch out for your baby,
Watch out for her now
She ain't no lady,
She's a stupid cow
She wears the trousers
She's got a tongue that stings
I know that woman
She's gonna do you in

She's high and mighty,
She wears a crown of steel
She'll dominate you,
She's got that special feel
She'll make you shiver
She'll make you reel and spin
I know that woman
She's gonna do you in

Don't tell her lies,
She's gonna find you out
You love to whisper,
You know she loves to shout
Don't talk back to her
Cos that's a mortal sin
I know that woman
She's gonna do you in

She's Not The Best

She's not the best
Pretty-ish
But like the rest
She does her best
To live up to the image
In the magazines
Pouting to the point
Of no return
Mouee 'til the cows come home

Home Virginia
Home

BOB GELDOF

She's So Modern

Ga ga ga ga
She's so 20th Century
She's so 1970's
She know the right things to say
She got the right clothes to wear
Cos she's a modern girl, oh yeah

And Suzie is a jewel,
She flashes when she smiles
She's cunning and she's clever
She's got the lowdown in her files.
Magenta is the best
You know she really makes me laugh
She's always tryin' her impressions
She wants to be a photograph,
I gotta say now

She's so 20th Century

And Jean confided to me
She's Mona Lisa's biggest fan,
She drew a moustache on her face
She's always seen her as a man.
And Charlie ain't no Nazi
She likes to wear her leather boots
Cos it's exciting for the veterans
And it's a tonic for the troops.

She's so 20th Century
She's so modern

Shine On

Shine on
Shine on me
Let your love
Shine down on me

I got a little bit of luck
When you walked through the door
Ah sexgod babe
I'm the one on the floor
Get me up babe
Get me up
And come over here
I need a little love juice
Trickling in my ear

I need a spiritual lift
And I need it now
I want outer space
Ah get me high
Get me high babe
I want to touch the sky
I need mojo-rise
I want to feel alive

Yea I know in your world
I'm just another face
Act like a slug
Make like a snake
Get up from the table
Lose your place
Waves come in
And leave no trace

BOB GELDOF

Sighs And Whispers

Sighs and whispers
Cries and whimpers
Over you

You said you were the only one
The one who broke all the rules
The one who's seen it all before
The one who wouldn't fall for fools
But as the night wore on a little bit
And the howling wind came down
What seemed so easy then
Doesn't seem so easy now

It's all a

Sigh and a whisper
A cry and a whimper
Cry me a river
Nothing new

And now the trees are bare
Stripped naked just like you
Silhouetted by the glare
Of an equally naked truth
The howling wind that stripped them
And the yellow street light shine
Leaves one thing to be decided
Is it your darkness or mine?

When it's just

Sighs and whispers
Cries and whimpers
Over you

Cry me a whimper
Sigh me a river
And I'm blue

Silly Pretty Thing

C'mon get up, get dressed
The world is spinning
Full of kindly beings
The one you love will love you back
And no-one's spoiling anything
Everything's just right
It makes you want to fill your lungs and sing
And ooh
You silly pretty little thing

C'mon get up, get dressed
Another perfect day of spring is here
Hurry up, c'mon get up
A soft wind's idly pushing past my ear
And water, clouds and lambs
Are tumbling over through the bursting fields
And ooh...
You silly pretty little thing

Last night the moon got drunk
and dropped his clothes down
on the empty streets
He danced a moon song
dancing 'cross the stars
before he had to go to sleep
And back down here the lovers gazed
And found they couldn't even speak
And ooh...
You silly pretty little thing

Oh I know there's some out there who'll always say
we're simply being naïve
But we believe in all that stuff like
Love and gentleness and peace
So today's the day we're going to come out
And declare our victory
Just you and me and that...
Silly pretty little thing

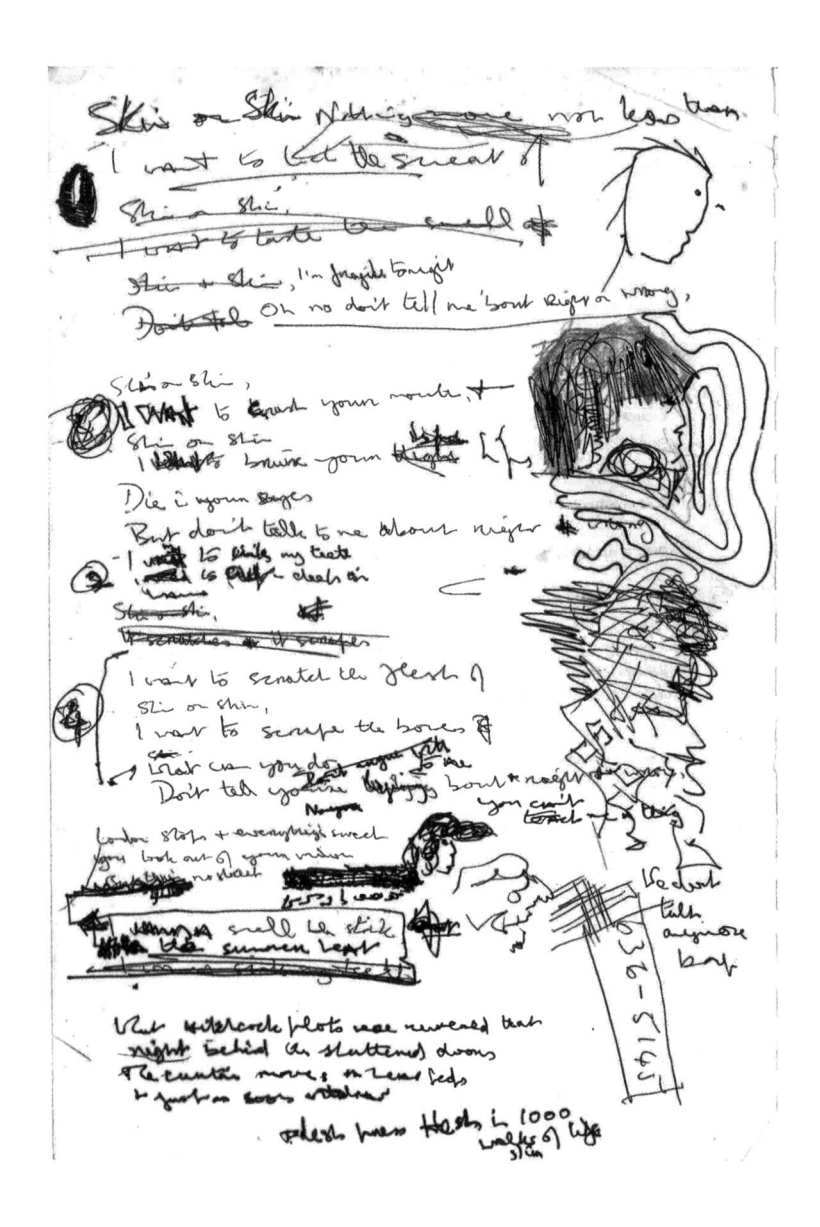

'SKIN ON SKIN' EARLY DRAFT OF LYRICS

Skin On Skin

Skin on Skin
Nothing more nor less than
Skin on skin
I want to lick the sweat off
Skin on skin
But don't talk to me about right or wrong

Skin on skin
I want to cut in deep in
Skin on skin
I need to sink my teeth in
Skin on skin
But don't talk to me about right or wrong

Skin on skin
I want to crush your mouth
And skin on skin
I want to bruise your lips
Tell me what do you know about right or wrong

Skin on skin
I want to scratch your flesh
And skin on skin
I need to scrape the bones of
Skin on skin
You can't teach me a thing about right or wrong

London stops
And everything's sweet
You look out of your window
But there's no street
The cars are gone
The night is dead
And the dogs have lost their growl
And the air seems stale
Cos the lions caged
It whimpers low
But the beast has been tamed

BOB GELDOF

So where's the riot
It's much too quiet
And my breath tastes like
Rotten feet
There's chatter from my window
But it seems so dead
And there's no one talking
But some talking heads
Yes, tonight we go to sleep
With the lullaby sound of buildings falling down

Hey d'ya hear the scratch of skin on skin
Hey d'ya feel the scrape of bone on bone

Things get tight, close to the bone
We feel fragile tonight
We don't like us much
But we can stay warm at least for an hour or two

Skin on skin
I need to scratch and bleed it
Skin on skin
Just the touch and feel of
Skin on skin
We don't talk anymore about right or wrong

Skin on skin
I want to smell the stink of
Skin on skin
Hot in the summer heat and
Skin on skin
I never open my mouth about right or wrong

So Strange

I was bleeding before I saw the blood
I was screaming but I soon woke up
On that night, on that night with you
I realized it was gonna be me or you

And it made me feel strange

So I knelt down and said my prayers that night
The fog was closing in on what remained of the light
On that night, on that night with you
I heard the wild dogs howling at the distant moon

Ooh and it made me feel strange

You told me you had arranged
For something special and strange
But suddenly I saw your eyes
And realised that you were quite insane

And when the dawn came I listened hard for your breath
You once told me
The bottom line of life is death
On that night, on that night with you
I realised it was gonna be me or you

And it made me feel strange
So strange

[Handwritten lyrics manuscript:]

Let the soil be your soft pillow
Grassy blankets keep you warm
Let the lazy breezes cool you
Let the blue sky keep you from all harm
Let the wind keep ~~push~~ your ~~body~~ memory
Let it blow across the land
Let the rain ~~keep~~ refresh your spirit
Let the damp earth hold your hand

Memory is sometimes perfect
Sometimes clearer than the light
You can wade + wallow through it
In the hollow of the night
La du du × 4.

I can see your ~~pale~~ white - tired face
Pale ghosts flit through empty streets
These are Christs born of another faith
+ No christ will ~~be~~ beneath you
Now the evening sun is rising
Lying flat on wintry fields
It carries, carries on its restless wind
The sound of ~~the~~ 50 church bells pealing

The Soft Soil

Let the soil be your soft pillow
The grassy blanket keep you warm
Let the leafy branches cool you
And the blue skies keep you from all harm
Let the wind keep fresh your memory
Let it blow across the land
Let the rain refresh your spirit
Let the damp earth hold your hand

Memory is sometimes perfect
Sometimes clearer than the light
You can wade and wallow through it
In the hollows of the night

And I can see your white and tired faces
Pale ghosts flitting through empty streets
There are Christs here of another faith
And no Christ will be beneath them

Now the evening sun is racing on
Lying flat on wintry fields
It carries on its restless winds
The sounds of fifty church bells peeling

And all the bells you've ever heard
Are ringing out for what you've done
Like all the dreams in all the world
You're shining reckless like the sun

And in the moment of your madness
In the centre of that storm
You understood it takes the same time
For man to die as to be born
Someday, maybe
When it gets them down
They will understand your bodies
Have pulled them up
As they went down

BOB GELDOF

And all the hope in all the world was
weighing down on top of you

So come on
Show me what to do
I'll follow you
Down this road
And try to learn from you
This may not mean a lot to you
It means a lot to me

Your breath will still be breathing softly
In a night time filled with stars
Drifting like a dream in sleep
Softly beating in your heart

Someone's Looking At You

On a night like this
I deserve to get kissed
At least once or twice
You come over to my place
Screaming blue murder,
Needing someplace to hide.
Well, I wish you'd keep quiet,
Imaginations run riot,
In these paper-thin walls.
And when the place comes ablaze
With a thousand dropped names
I don't know who to call.
I got a friend over there
In the government block
And he knows the situation
And he's taking stock,
I think I'll call him up now
Put him on the spot, tonight.

They saw me there in the square
When I was shooting my mouth off
About saving some fish.
Now could that be construed
As some radicals views
Or some liberals wish.
And it's so hot outside,
And the air is so sweet,
And when the pressure drop is heavy
I don't wanna hear you speak.
You know most killing is committed at 90 degrees.
When it's too hot to breathe
And it's too hot to think.

There's always someone looking at you.

BOB GELDOF

And I wish you'd stop whispering.
Don't flatter yourself,
Nobody's listening.
Still it makes me nervous,
Those things you say.
You may as well
Shout it from the roof
Scream it from your lungs
Spit it from your mouth
'Cos there's a spy in the sky
There's a noise on the wire
There's a tap on the line
And for every paranoid's desire...
There's always someone looking at you.

The Song Of The Emergent Nationalist

Over there across the river
Coming in over the sea
Flying in the salt sky
Washed up on the beach
Over across the sand dunes
Up among the broken reeds
Way up in the branches
Higher up than the trees
If you listen hard you can hear them
Blowing in on the breeze
Saying come back
Baby come back

There's a place you can go when you're empty
The older you are and you get
If you concentrate you will catch them
But sometimes you have to forget
And as the years make the hearing harder
There's a secret place that I know
Take my hand across this blasted land
We can listen to them sigh and moan
Whisper come back

Where is your culture
It's been stolen
Where are your ideals
They've been stolen
Where is your nation
It's been stolen
Where is your language
Gone
Where are your traditions
Robbed
Where is your future
It's been stolen
Who are you now
We don't know
We're nothing now we are gone

BOB GELDOF

But a whispered secret voice says
No we have only withdrawn
We are shadows of what we were
But we're a long, long shadow
And in that shadow is our shape
And in that shape is our name
And where we hide it is dark
But in the dark it is warm
We are born in this dark and we're safe
When it's time
We'll come again

Straight Up

Hey, she'll set the world alight
She's looking lost with life
But no-one's on fire
And still she burns
She waits her turn

Straight up.

Sometimes at least it seems
She hears the whole place scream
But she finds sleep
With light hand relief
She's going deep

She holds no convictions
Which means she never doubts

Day falls into night
She draws the blind
Calls it a day
And when she wakes
Sees nothing's changed

Straight up.

She just stands there waiting
Waiting for something
Anything at all
Nothing at all
Not at all.

BOB GELDOF

'SUMMERS EVENING' EARLY DRAFT OF LYRICS

Summers Evening (London '05)

Up here the air is cleaner
The burning city seems to breathe
Exhausted afternoon lies sighing
For the night

A gentle jazz note rising
Traffic hissing disappears
Like a burbling stream
Vanishing off-screen
The city empties
Somewhere unseen

A final flaring
Angry sun
Sinks glaring down below
The high-rise line

And on my roof
My fevered skin
Is stroked by evenings
Velvet limbs
The night is beckoning
Like a bride
To moonrise

Then suddenly
Night falls fast
The evening stars
Dark
At last

BOB GELDOF

Sweet Thing

Sweet thing
You make my gums bleed
You're my pretty thing
Because I love you

I'm gonna love you Monday
You're the start of my week
Tuesday, Wednesday, Thursday
Man we're hitting a peak
But I love you best on Friday
Cos you're my weekend freak
My little sweet thing

They're beaming hope out baby on the local airwaves
So tune into the one that offers hope and can save you
I love you in the morning when I wake and you're shaving
O my sweet thing
A wo, wo, wo
A yea, yea, yea

We're going to keep on driving
'Til the end of the night
It's hopeless but I'm helpless
You're the beam in my light
There's a rumour you're a tumour on my lovestick alright
My little sweet thing

I'm gonna call the cops up cos it just isn't right
The world looks so much better
When I've got you in my sights
Tear up all those old plans
And let's light up that night
My sweet thing

Systematic 6-Pack

I gotta brand new automatic, systematic 6-pack
Flat pack
Gotta get my body back on track
Cos everything is going south

I wanna time shifting, face lifting, tight butt, no gut
Trout pouting, collagenically botox mouthing
Everything is hanging down
Systematic 6-pack; you're 58 and a half

Freeze dried
Don't it make you cryogenically preserved
And isn't it absurd
You're going to be conserved in ice
Nice!

Give me a sexual Niagara
Little diamond blue pill
Gotta get Viagra
A drag, still I wanna shag
Get hard, too hard
You're 58 and a half

O man!

BOB GELDOF

Talking In Code

Why are you talking in code?
You talk so loud sometimes we don't understand
C'mon give us a sign
Wave us a flag or flash me an eye
Cos I need you tonight
I need you right now
I got sweat on my mind
But you're taking your time
Yeah kiss where it stings c'mon show me a time

But when you talk in code and you talk in signs
Wave those hands
And you flash those eyes
I don't understand when you blind me with science
You talk in code
Talking keep talking

Decipher me now
Describe me an arc with a low point or two
Ah cough me a code
Astonish me dear with a new point of view
Yes it's all in your hands
The Wristwatch Frisco is in action again
Ah well I like you I think
It varies so much sometimes it really depends on
If you talk in code

And then if A = B
Sometimes what you say isn't all that it seems
And if C = 3
Inscrutable view with a new slant on things
Ah semaphore girl
I love the taste of you dressed up in green
But you're talking in code
I don't understand but I won't make a scene

Cos when you talk in code...

Thinking Voyager 2 Type Things

This is the moment that we come alive
I'm handing out the breath and the kiss
I'm electric with the snap and the crackle of creation
I'm mixing up the mud with the spit
So rise up Brendan Behan and like a drunken Lazarus
Let's traipse the high bronze of the evening sky
Like crack crazed kings.

Voyager 2 where are you now
Looking back at home and weeping
Cold and alone in the dark void
Winding down and bleeping
Ever dimmer, ever thinner
Feebly cheeping in the solar winds
I'll turn you up

Sail on sail on sail on
On past the howling storms
Through electric orange skies
And blinding methane rain
Sail on
I'll turn you up.

Never bring me down to earth again
Let me blaze a trail of glory across the sky
Let me traipse across it's golden high
Let me marvel in wonder and unfettered gaze
At the bigness and implausibility of being
Yes stretch out your hands into infinity you human things
Past blind moons and ice cream worlds
You hurl your metal ball of dull intelligence
And show us all our fragile grip
As we too track with you
Slower but no less insistent
Like the only fertile seed
In the barren vault of being
Sail on
Hurtling towards the waiting womb of empty worlds
Waiting for the final primary come of life
I'll turn you up

BOB GELDOF

And I'm thinking big things
I'm thinking about mortality
I'm thinking it's a cheap price that we pay for existence
This is the moment that we come alive
This is the breath and this is the kiss

Now we're in Paris
In the ball gowns
In the high heels
In the snow
And we're spinning round Versailles in a Volkswagen Beetle
That we'd hired for the day
(At the cheap rate)
The room without the shower was cold again
"Are we already middle-aged", she said
And I said "I feel nothing
I feel like a jelly-fish".
"Maybe it's the Portuguese Men-O-Pause", she joked
And she laughed her brittle head
And we went back to bed
And I've been thinking about these things
I've been thinking about Voyager 2
And this is the moment that we come alive

This Heartless Heart

They won't break you
With that heartless heart
They'll never shake you
With that heartless heart

She's the kinda girl
Who like to show the boys
There's only one around here
Really makes a noise
She'll do ya
Ooh yea

She's the kinda woman's
Kinder to be cruel
I see her now and then
She's always trying to fool ya
Ooh yea
Who could believe that she's saying
All these things tonight
Who would believe that the world
would go crazy tonight
Will this heartless heart
Tear us apart

They won't change you
No, they won't break you
Not with that heartless heart

But please stop telling me
We got to
We need to
We must do
We can do
I'm tired of hearing remedies
For things that really never needed cures

Who would believe that she's saying all this stuff tonight
Who would believe that we're listening to this crap tonight
Will this heartless heart
Tear us apartment

This Is My Room

I can sleep alone
I know how
I stay here on my own
And now.

I wake from sleep with little rest
It's 10 by 9 and in a mess
A window shut but facing west
A worn out rug, an old address
And
This is my room
Yes
This is my room

I often stay at home
I often sleep alone
I know how

BOB GELDOF

This Is The World Calling

I hear a heart beat
It's ringing out across the universe
It sounds so lost and lonely
It must come from somewhere deep inside of us
And the operator says
"All is calm
All is quiet
Close your eyes and sleep tonight"

This is the world calling
This is the earth
This is the world calling
This is us

I'm on a train now
I'm moving through the yellow fields of rape
There's so much beauty
I wished that I believed enough to pray
Then the operator says
"Spinning 'round you're wrapped in blue
There's no-one looks as good as you"

This is the world calling
This is us
And it goes on and on

What we going to do because it can't go on
Wrap me in your arms and keep me warm tonight

This is the world calling
God help us

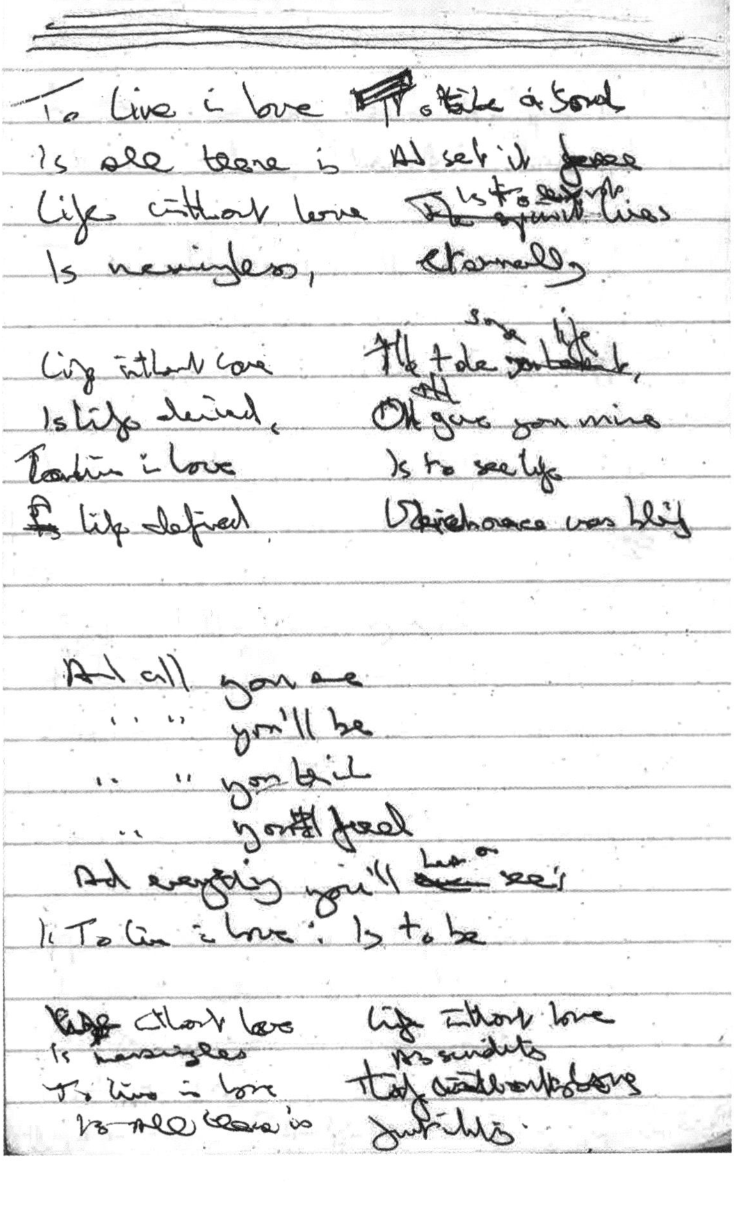

'TO LIVE IN LOVE' DRAFT OF LYRICS

BOB GELDOF

To Live In Love

To live in love
Is all there is
Life without love
Is meaningless

Life without love
Is life denied
To live in love
Is life defined

To take a life
Or I'll give you mine
Is to see life
Where life was blind

And all you are
And all you'll be
And all you think
And all you'll feel
And everything
You hear or see
To live in love
Is to be

Life without love
Absurdity
Life without love
Futility

'TONIGHT' EARLY DRAFT OF LYRICS

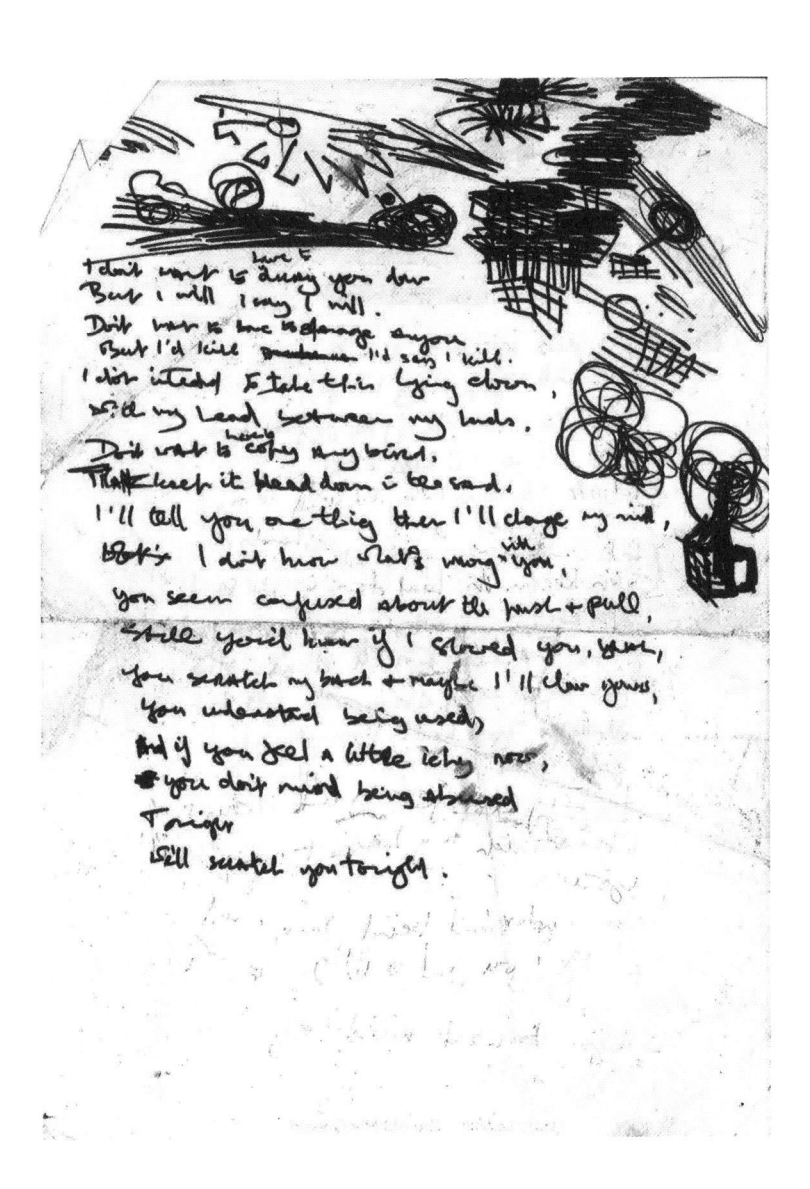

'TONIGHT' EARLY DRAFT OF LYRICS

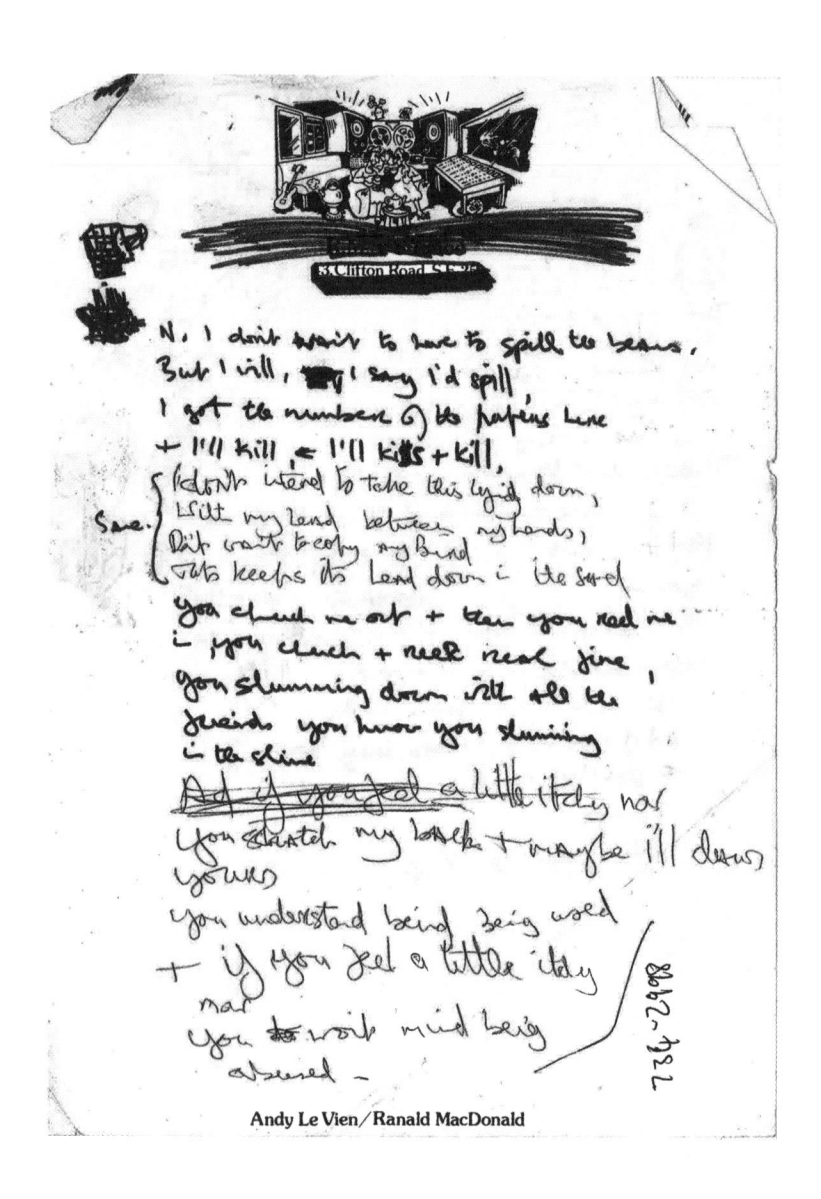

Tonight

Oh, I don't wanna have to take you out
But I will, said I will
Don't have to damage anyone
But I'd kill, kiss and kill
I don't intend to take this lying down
With my head between my hands, no
I don't intend to copy any bird
That keeps it's head stuck in the sand, oh

You scratch my back
And maybe I'll claw yours
You understand being used
And if you feel a little itchy now
You won't mind being abused

Tonight... the towers crumble
Tonight... the mountains fall
Tonight... no one stumbles
Tonight... no one stalls
Scratch it tonight

You don't wanna have to spill those beans
But you will, I said you will
You got the numbers of the papers here
And you will, kiss and spill
You chuck me out and then you reel me in
Oh you chuck and you reel real fine
You're slumming down with all those friends you got
You've been slumming in the slime

You scratch my back
And maybe I'll claw yours
You understand being used
And if you feel a little itchy now
You won't mind being abused

BOB GELDOF

Tonight... the towers crumble
Tonight... the mountain falls
Tonight... no one tumbles
Tonight... no one calls
Scratch it tonight

We're itching tonight
Scratch you tonight
All right all right
You want me tonight yeah
All right all right
Do it tonight
Sit tight
Fool me tonight

Too Late God

Too late
It's too late God
Didn't you get my message
Too late
It's too late God
Didn't you get my call
How long
How long con
Combien ans avant mon respond
Innocent
Un a cent a mort (or more)

Time flies
Like a brick
Sliding down my face like jelly roll
Try to hide
My belly slide
Half-way to being old

Things you do
Things you don't do
Things you do or don't will haunt you
It's harder to
Start anew
And I wouldn't if I could do

Fell in love
Fell out of love
Melted down like Chernobillyboil
Fell in love my turtle dove
Turtles fly too slow

Incarnate
Re-incarnate
Incarcerate me in my muddy hole
Won't come back
As a Rat
Wouldn't if I could do

BOB GELDOF

There I was
Here I am
A responsible citizen
A pillar of
All that's good
Put myself to sleep

Hormone twitch
Get the itch
Headfirst into male-o-menopause
Like a twat
Dye my thatch
Get an eighteen year old girl

Friends of mine
Leave their wives
For a top-down B.M.W.
They seemed sane yesterday
Life is really strange

Here we go
Here we go
Singing like some soccer hooligan
Call you back
When I'm at
70 years old

Too Late She Cried

Too late she cried
She got her anger from her mother's side
She broke down
And she died

Too much I thought
I struggled manfully
But was overwrought
A trapped fly
She got caught

And all of this is best avoided
The mountain climbed
The mountain climb
To all my friends who destroyed us
I'm marking time
Just marking time

Too much I thought
I struggled manfully
But was overwrought
Trapped flies
We got caught

See all of this is best avoided
The hours chime
They chime
To all our friends
Who destroyed us
I'm marking time
Just marking time

BOB GELDOF

Trash Glam Baby

O no
Another shit Saturday night
My jeans don't fit and the money's tight
Adele is working down at the charity shop
She's got a pair of boots in
So maybe she'll swop
For my Biba blouse
And my pink feather boa
Is shedding all its feathers
I don't wanna live no more
I got my diamante and my stick-on stars
I got my New York Dolls
I got my Spiders From Mars

Trash Glam Baby
It's a trash can world
You're a glitter ball honey
You're a glitter bomb
Dancing by yourself at the Moth Club tonight
And maybe getting burned
Dancing too close to the lights

In class they teach "World Civilizations"
I can't get my head around the whole situation
I mean how d'ja even have an adult conversation
Without talking about Trash Glam Nation

Yea I'm a Tank Top Terrorist
I'm making the scene
My fishnets gotten ladders
All along the seams
I'm yer basic vacant youth
If yis know what I mean
It ain't retro
It's just metro
2017

Another shit Saturday night
My jeans don't fit
And the money is tight

Truly, True Blue

When the red rose
Burst its blooming bud
And pouring out
Its thorny golden blood,
Over you,
I'll be
True blue

When the cold and brittle late October sky
Crystallizes, snaps and cracks then shatters over you
And the heat on Henry Street
Melts the tar beneath your feet
That bubbles up and then gets stuck to you
And the trees hang heavy with their fruit and rain
That hovers threateningly over you
Then I'll be
Truly true blue.

BOB GELDOF

Two Dogs

Two dogs
On the highway
They've had nothing to eat all week

They look at each other
One says "I wish I was born a cat"
The other says "Don't even think that!"

Two dogs laughing
Howling downtown
They snipe and snarl
They take leaks
They do dog stuff

They like to sniff at human crotches
They like the effect
(Deep in the doggy doo-doo)

They're really hungry
It's lunchtime
(Deep in the doggy doo doo)
Out of the alley on the left hand side comes a man
They don't know it, but HE hasn't eaten all week
(Deep in the doggy doo-doo)

They're in the same boat
Two dogs, one man
He's elite, they think
What they don't know is that he's been watching them all week
And his bite is worse than their bark
(Deep in the doggy doo-doo)

It's a dog's life
It's a man's world

Under Their Thumb (Is Under My Thumb)

Under their thumb
Kicked and beaten like an angry rabid dog
Under their thumb
Squashed and squeezed like a dried-up, rinsed out worm
You can't do a thing
Best lie still 'til you wait your turn
Can't do a thing
Your day will come
You're under their thumb

Under their thumb
And now you feel you're not alone
Under their thumb
And now you feel the pressure zone
You can't do a thing
Revenge is sweet but it's sugar free
Can't do a thing
Your day will come
Now you're under their thumb

BOB GELDOF

Up All Night

Up all night
Ooh za za
Ooo I was up all night

African jungle
Big city street
(Bee-beepin', beep-beep yeah)
The only real difference is in
The people you meet

It's an agreeable town
It's neat and sedate
(Car parkin', car park yeah)
Why even the muggers
Get off the streets by eight
Then stay...

Polite and well spoken
Well-heeded and well sane
(Zoot suitin', zoot suit yeah)
They know they're alive
When they start to feel pain

V DEEP, 1982

The Vegetarians Of Love

Whoa here they come
The Vegetarians of Love
They're all friends of mine now
The Vegetarians of Love
They're doing real good things
They don't eat meat
And they're joining clubs
I like them a lot now
Those Vegetarians of Love

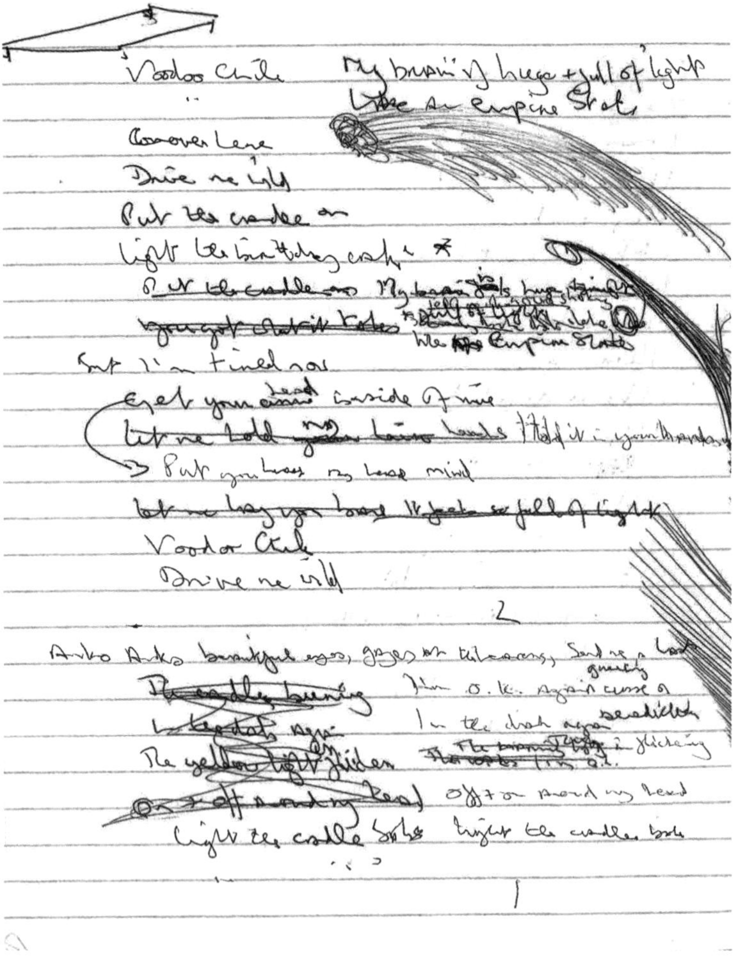

Voodoo Child

My brain is huge + full of light
Like an Empire State

Drive me wild

Put the candle on

Light the birthday cake

But I'm tired now

Voodoo Child
Drive me wild

Voodoo Child

Voodoo child
Come over here
Drive me wild

Put the candle on
Light the birthday cake
My brain is huge
And full of light
Like an Empire State
I'm tired now

Put your head inside of mine
Hold it in your hands
Put your heart inside my mind
Hold it in your hands

Voodoo child
Drive me wild

Anko, Anko
Beautiful eyes
Gazing at the heavens
Send me a last greeting
A curse or benediction

Light the candle babe

In halls of gold
Long times ago
I watched your naked fear
In marbled baths
From ancient urns
I saw you fade in tears
The choir chants
The incense burns
The tambourine beats time
Bronzed obelisks
Guard the priests

Who keep the sacred fire
And voodoo child
You drive me wild

The night is soft
The air is sweet
Time tolls its tiny beat
You indolently spread
Your naked limbs
Around the heat

What's that you're crying about
Come over here and whisper it
If you don't want to shout

Light the candle babe
It's getting dark
And I can't see
Voodoo child
You drive me wild

Here comes the night
And I'm too tired

BOB GELDOF

Walking Back To Happiness

Dark skies the rain falling down on my head tonight
But I looked up + I could clearly see the moon,
For a second I thought I was somewhere romantic like Mississippi
But I was walking down by Chelsea bayou.

It takes you by surprise the places you find yourself in
One minute you're here, next minute you're somewhere else
+ then you're gone.
If it wasn't for a well-placed sense of direction.
You could lose your head + simply carry on.

Walking back to happiness.
(Like Helen Shapiro did

me + Helen arm in arm.

BOB GELDOF

Walking Back to Happiness

Dark skies are falling down on my head tonight
But I looked up and I could clearly see that moon
For a second I thought I was somewhere
romantic like Mississippi
But I was walking down Chelsea Bayou
It takes you by surprise the places you find yourself in
One minute you're here
Next minute you're there
And then you're gone
If it wasn't for a well placed sense of direction
You could lose your head and simply carry on
Walking back to happiness
Like Helen Shapiro did
Me and Helen
Arm in arm

Foghorns boom the daylight gloom descends
Too soon on wintry afternoons
That frightened heart of youth is with me now
Still staring out from its upstairs room
And you can take any road you wish to walk
You can swim to the furthest shore
Or you can be like Joan of Arc babe
And plug into the planets core
And go walking back to happiness

I feel happy already watch me smile
See me laughing
Later on see me cry

And as it gets colder and the night wears on a little bit
I cool down yes I cool my heels
I remember my father and me down on the East Pier
He's pointing at the ships saying they're leaving here
Where do they go?
Where do they go?
Eastward Ho
Eastward Ho

Yes I remember my father
Standing on the edge of the Pier
Pointing with his finger Eastward Ho
We were walking back to happiness
And here we go

BOB GELDOF

Walking Downtown

It's strange here, it's funny in a way
Is it the night air makes it this way

10,000 streets under an orange sky
And a million stories in a fully clothed city
And I've heard every one of them
[Not only that]
I've been every one of them
[Not only that]
Nobody's interested anyway

This place stinks like Chicago
[Junkietown, Junkietown]
It smells of cabbage and grey water
[Junkietown, Junkietown]
There's fear round here
It stinks the place up
Seeping out through the cracks and basements
But I'm walking out
No I'm not afraid
The grass is greener on the newest graves

When the last jive had been jiven
Those left alive just upped and risen
From the damp walls and clammy tongues
And the quickly cooling sweat of lousy sex
Huh?
[6345789]
Yeah that's my number
[6345789]
Why don't you come by some time
And you know, dial it up

Some days you wonder how these things begin
Don't look, it'll happen anyway
When one thing leads to maybe 6 or 5
You eat well, you sleep well, and that's saying something
    these days

LIVE DEMO, EXTRA TRACK ON THE REMASTERED, IN THE LONG GRASS, 1984

Walking Downtown

I don't want to think like this
I wanna think like an animal
[Junkietown, Junkietown]
I exist, therefore I'm happy
[Junkietown, Junkietown]
If you come here to look for your world
Please leave your muscles with the hat check girl
Cos everybody in the Eyelash Set
Start their hearts with whatever's left
[6345789]
That's the number, say it again
[6345789]
You gotta make note of it
Some time when you drop by
You know, dial it up

Walking Downtown

Sometimes I feel like I'm the first person to set foot in America
Who looked around and thought
What the fuck is this?

BOB GELDOF

(Watch Out For) The Normal People

She keeps her lover on ice,
She keeps a fire in the grate,
He's got a movement in his cellar,
He's a danger to the state.
Watch out for the normal people
There's more of us than there's of you
Well you're a really lucky bugger,
That you haven't been discovered,
Ain't that true

She has a genuine fridge
He has a night on the town
Their receptions too good
They've got 2 up and 2 down
Watch out for the normal people

Normal can and normal will (Uncle Jack)
When normal Jack meets normal Jill (Auntie Jill)
A normal wedding on a normal pill (take their pills)
They bought a normal house on your
Average, scenic, normal hill,
They live there still...

He's got a family connection,
She got an uncle in steel,
He gets depressed in the evening
She thinks she knows how he feels.

When I Was Young

Live fast
Be a spark and glow a while
You'll be dead a long, long time

Be a shooting star
And in one mad moment
Burning bright
Light the night
And make us stand in awe

Live fast
Be a supernova
Explode now while you can
Then flashing in the pan
Be a streak of red
Against the grey
Do it young
Don't let time slip away
And make us real
And feel
And see
Your beauty
Live fast.

When I was young
I would do a million things
Dreaming up a thousand schemes
I would change the world each night

I would tear the stars apart
Confusion tore that pounding heart
With certainty that things weren't right

I'd read all that student stuff
Read it till I'd had enough
Then making up my own mind
Think it
Feel it

BOB GELDOF

I believed I'd never die
When I was young

When I was young
Hopes were built like shining spires
Reaching up and spearing skies
That rained their bitter tears around

I remember all these things and more
I believed I'd never die
When I was young

Baby, baby, baby when the whole world turns around
Baby, baby, baby keeps both feet on the ground
Baby, baby, baby when there's nothing left to do
Then baby, baby, baby I hold on tight to you
Cos there ain't no rear view mirror in my car
I ain't looking back
Not very far

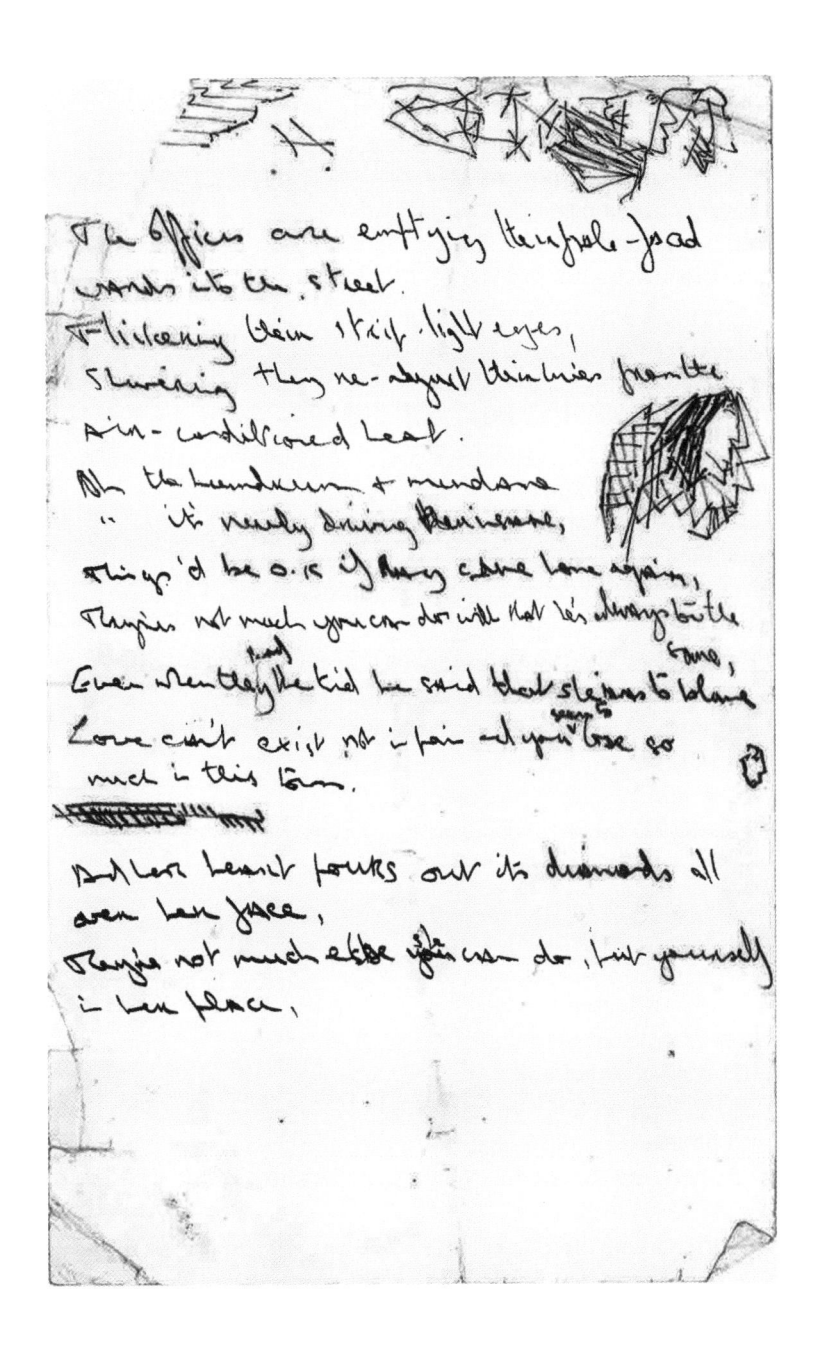

'WHEN THE NIGHT COMES' EARLY DRAFT OF LYRICS

BOB GELDOF

When The Night Comes

The offices are emptying
Their pale-faced wards into the street,
Flickering their strip-light eyes,
Shivering they readjust their lives
From the air-conditioned heat.
The humdrum and mundane
Is nearly driving them insane.
But you get hooked so quick to anything
Even your chains,
You're crouching in your corner
'Til they open up your cage.

And when the night comes
It'll help you disappear
And when the night comes
Forget about the day that brought you here.

Frankie takes the train and makes it home in time to
    catch the evening news,
Opening a can of beans he learns the world has turned
    without much help from him.
Hey Frank, why not get drunk tonight?
Hey Frank, I think it'll be alright,
You'll be too far gone to notice when the neighbours
    start complaining,
But they're used to it by now, every day's the same.

And when the night comes,
He might get on the phone,
She's a stuck-up bitch,
But she lives on her own,
And he heard her talking dirty to the girls the other day,
And she knew that he had heard her and she looked
"as if to say"
And then later up in marketing while going through the files,
She bent a little too far down, then turned around and smiled.

He got her number,
He got the phone,
He dialled the number,
He heard the tone.
He said "Tonight's the night that I've been waiting for,
Oh I know you've seen me worship you from afar,
And I might tell you that I love you and I will but just for
Tonight, one night, alright tonight".

In his three piece cunning camouflage
Nobody can guess what Frankie's thinking,
Last night she said "I don't know if I'm drowning
Maybe it's because I'm sinking."
He said "It'll be okay
I'll get outta here one day"
And she said "Frankie, you're no different from any of the rest,
They've nailed you to that table and chained you to your desk."
But when the night comes...

And when the night comes
It'll help you disappear
And when the night comes
Forget about the day that brought you here.

BOB GELDOF

Wind Chill Factor (Minus Zero)

*'It's one of those days where I don't like myself
But I get along with me O.K.
I'll slip beneath these sheets and shiver here awhile
I find this happening more frequently these days.'*

Largely the struggle was done. Heaving yourself out of the mire of beginning, that titanic struggle to get born, get known, recognised, achieve escape velocity and GO. Exhausting. That was just Ireland. Then becoming unknown again in Britain and starting all over once more.

But now the records had been golden and platinumed and number one'd and awarded, the shows were rafter-stuffed and people screamed embarrassingly, and we were pop stars and sort of used to it and it was like our official 'job'. The only one most of us had ever had, really.

And though I'd often read about it, I hadn't quite believed it – I was fed up. There was a part of me that, cliché-like, wasn't mad for this at all. It's not that it wasn't what I'd wanted. It's not that I didn't understand how improbable the situation was. It's not that I didn't thrill to the perks, upsides and the glimpse of life beyond the velvet rope. It was just ... oh I don't know ... some weird combination of unease and pressure which fed the exhaustion, paranoia, boredom (oddly) and the inevitable large dollops of the 'fraud syndrome'. Y'know ... any day now they're going to find you out. You're just too exposed. Anyone that obvious is almost always naked in the eyes of the unbeliever. For the others you are, momentarily anyway, a Golden One upon whom all personal projections are permitted.

For yourself, you must acclimatise. Learn to hide in plain sight.

My thinking was to be counter-intuitive and hide nothing. Talk endlessly and I thought openly, and that would stop 'mystique' or 'mystery' accruing about the 'star' figure, the accumulation of which mystique would 'like the bark of a cork tree' ultimately smother the individual concerned. Except that didn't work either. The believer simply hears the mundane and unexceptional as being somehow different.

The 'star' thing had never interested me and I was no good at it anyway. But I had wanted to be famous. There is a difference. I had been able to use the Fame as I said I would, 'to talk about the things that bothered me'. The songs were doing that, and I had played at a couple of benefit events and spoken in Trafalgar Square about the things I thought needed to be addressed. But what needed to be addressed right now was what the fuck was going on inside my head. What exactly was wrong with me?

I was 27. I OWNED MY OWN HOUSE, FFS!!! Small, sure, but outright! I lived with the prettiest girl in the world. People were nice to me on the street cos they saw me on Top Of The Pops or whatever. One summer's night I turned on the car radio and every station was playing one of our songs! WOW! I hung with 'the stars'. I was invited to the premieres. They sent limos for me. I felt a right fucking eejit in them (head screams – FRAUD!!), but hey – better than the shit Renault 4L of a year ago.

But there was a very real fear there. One flop and you're gone. A life constantly lived on that ephemeral precipice is one lived in a world of broken sleep and a grand fear of loss. I often couldn't write. And if I did write, what would it be about now that the first urges of dam-bursting catharsis had been spent? And what if those songs when (please dear god) they did come weren't hits? "What then?" cried Plato's ghost, "What then?" (W.B. Yeats).

The clue is in the name, I suppose. 'Wind Chill Factor (Minus Zero)'. Paranoia is a cold thing. Like the end of love. This tune drips "fucked up". I'm definitely not in a good place. The track is overwrought and over-produced but that's just us with these new-fangled ARP synthesisers playing around. *The Fine Art Of Surfacing*, we got the name of album 3 from this song but actually I'd taken the phrase from an article I'd read in Psychology Today. Why was I reading that? Read the song!

Ref. also the same record …'Someone's Looking At You', 'Having My Picture Taken', 'Nothing Happened Today', 'I Don't Like Mondays', 'Diamond Smiles', etc. etc. … These are not happy songs. We were at 'the top'. We were. We were actually at the toppest of the tops of Mount Pop. It's what we'd wanted. What we'd worked for and it's a cliché and I'm not eliciting sympathy here … but man, it's a rare oxygen up there. Your head gets light but it's hard to breathe.

BOB GELDOF

Wind Chill Factor (Minus Zero)

I took a tube train through the subway systems.
I rode those tunnels like a six foot mole.
I came back out and I was gasping for air.
I made it to your place, I was praying you'd be home.
We really shouldn't be alone tonight.
Let's go to a movie where everybody fights
But in the end there's dancing, songs, and smiles
You need lots of smiles... when the

Wind chill factor's minus zero
Wind chill factor's minus 10 below.
Wind chill factor's minus zero
Wind chill factor. There you go.

It's one of those days where I don't like myself
But I get along with me O.K.
I'll slip beneath these sheets and shiver here awhile
I find this happening more frequently these days.
Still... I practice nightly, I try to keep ahead.
This art of surfacing is all but dead.
But I'll keep coming up, with time enough to breathe,
I take what I need... when the
Wind chill factor's minus zero

Do you agree (no)
With anything (no)
Do you believe (no)
In anything (no)
At all (no)

You know when winter comes to visit these big cities,
And the wind starts howling through the elevator shafts.
Well, our love is like one of those older, colder buildings.
My concrete's cracked and I begin to feel the draught.

You start to laugh (no)
You say you've won (no)
It's just I lost (no)

That's not the same (no)
I'll hobble to my corner and review the situation.
And we'll settle finally for some form
Of deep freeze
Hibernation......

Now the wind chill factor's minus zero

BOB GELDOF

The Women In My Life

The women in my life
Mother, daughters, wife
Ex-wives and lovers
Sisters, friends and others
In almost equal measure
Give me pain and pleasure
The women in my life

The women in my life
Have almost broken me
But still awoken me
To possibilities
Of places I'd have never seen
Or people I'd have never been
Without the women in my life

And though my many friends
Are almost always men
Some dealt the toughest hands
And surveyed the roughest lands
And while together life is sweet
If not exactly Easy St.,
Still somehow incomplete
Without the women in our lives

Words From Heaven

Don't be confused
You're back in time again
It's funny but it's true
They state your case
Praise your name and the last place
Where you lived without a trace
Except that face that shone for you
That faith belonged to you
It saw you through again
Those eyes of Danish blue
Set in pain
We all thought you were so brave
When they laughed called you insane
But now they're saying
These words came from heaven

I'm happy for you
We've got to laugh again
Cos when they thought they'd you
Stretched on racks
You refused to answer back
You sat still you never cracked
Till they backed down in front of truth
And now they say
These words came from heaven
Straight to you.

BOB GELDOF

Yeah, Definitely

If I fall down on my knees
And my tear-stained cheeks say "Please..."
Well yeah

And if you take me
From this world
Of lies and pain and hurt
Well yeah

From your mouth you breathe
The breath of Summer's kiss
The magic words of calm
Come pouring from your lips

Hey babe come here quick
My head is pounding
My mind is sick
Yeah

Everybody I know said you must be joking
When they saw me with you
They laughed until they choked
Say Yeah, Yeah, Yeah

And I know when it gets too much
I'll lean on you
My velvet crutch
Oh yeah

Hey you little pretty thief
You stole my fear
And gave me peace
of mind
I say yeah, yeah, yeah

BOB GELDOF

Young And Sober

In the year of '55
When I was but a child
I felt the Lord settle on my shoulder
Throughout those childish days
He would guide my guileless ways
For I was young and sober

Then in the year of '65
A troubled life midst troubled times
And the Lord just sat there on my shoulder
But I wished that life was other
Or that I could be another
But I was me
And I was young and sober

Now in the year of '75
Was when I sang myself alive
And the Lord just sat there whistling on my shoulder
So I stood up and I sang
And that's when my life began
And I was young and sober

But in the year of '85
We watched the millions starve and die
And the Lord perched like a vulture on my shoulder
So we sent some bread and water
Tried our best to stop the slaughter
For we were young and sober

Then in the year of '95
I loved my faithless wife
And the Devil must have muttered on her shoulder
Cos she left me for another
Whom I once had thought my brother
And I grew drunk and older

Still in the year of '05
With my beautiful new wife

BOB GELDOF

And the Lord just sat there smiling on our shoulders
Well we drank from life's rich cup
Watched the children growing up
For she had made me once again
Young and sober!

Index of first lines

A storm breaks over our head	35
All the birdies swimming in the sea	235
Alright I'm leaving	32
And these are hard times	137
And you can drive on Damo	109
As soon as I wake up every day	105
Baby in the dead of the night	242
Baby's going down again	50
Banana republic, septic Isle	57
Bankers gone and stolen all my money	58
Battersea Morning it's bright in the early dawning	59
Before the day begins I lie awake	62
Blow hateful wind cold on faithless skin	66
Bright lights of Dublin are twinkling tonight	74
Bring in the dog	266
Calling… In my head its calling	51
Can't stop and face the facts	75
Charmed lives, nothing much to do tonight	78
C'mon get up, get dressed	293
David called me up yesterday	89
Dark skies are falling down on my head tonight	336
Days are long, the nights are too	103
Did they never tell you 'bout it baby	63
Did you slip the noose when the beast broke loose	112
Dog days fall without saying anything	230
Don't be confused, you're back in time again	351
Don't wanna live all by myself	234
Down at Hotel 75	147
Down at the street around half past nine	80
Drag me down in colours pink and gold	107
Europe looked ugly the very last time that I saw her	117
Every morning 'bout the break of day	135
Everybody I meet wants to knock me down	178
Everybody's gonna catch their death	171
Everybody's got a hole to fill	25
First time that I saw you	84
Ga ga ga ga she's so 20th Century	290
Get a grip baby, get a grip on yourself	126
Hand me down a strong panacea	219

He bought and sold a video	142
He rodent into town	99
Here comes Johnny Nogood	186
Here comes the night again, babe	83
Here she comes like a Queen all through the wintertime	31
Here she comes walking down the street	144
Here they go, lying again	213
Here's to you and all our friends	146
Hey baby there's a storm coming up	92
Hey Mr. Mojo with your mop-top hair	224
Hey, she'll set the world alight	305
I been drinking like a blowfish	67
I can be your friend	125
I can sleep alone, I know how	315
I don't get my kicks no more from cake or lemonade	191
I don't mind if you go	133
I don't want to listen	157
I got a brand-new car	255
I got a little brittle heart	81
I got home last night about 8	245
I got off the 45A somewhere around the new estates	149
I gotta brand new automatic, systematic 6-pack	309
I hear a heart beat	316
I heard Tarzan outside playing on the Jungle Blues	151
I know you're pretty and you're young	38
I meant to say, I thought you knew	233
I never loved Eva Braun (Oh no?)	168
I thought I'd write a letter	187
I took a tube train through the subway systems	348
I want you	169
I was bleeding before I saw the blood	297
I was reading in New Zealand about Ian Smith	42
I was walking down the street	264
I'd tear down the sky	239
I'll take another photograph	48
I'm driving on the road Hitler built	277
I'm gonna Boomtown	72
I'm not disconnected	196
I'm tired of listening to you	152
I've been living all my life in a Ratlife	274
I've been reading your sex magazines	222

I've never seen the place look greener	36
If I fall down on my knees	352
If I stand up on the wall again	265
If you see her say hello	22
In abandoned empty rooms	91
In her £2.00 coat	188
In the year of '55 when I was but a child	353
It was cold that night when the crows flew west	60
It was last night baby when I caught your eye	211
It was late and it was Tuesday	263
It's 3, here's me	177
It's been a good life, I can't complain	179
It's Christmastime and there's no need to be afraid	102
It's hard times trying to make a living	153
It's strange here, it's funny in a way	338
Jeanne saved my soul again last night	19
Jungle Joe say to Uncle Sam	77
Late last night she called me on the telephone	286
Later on that evening when I thought I'd had enough	45
Lay me down by some fields and streams	121
Let the soil be your soft pillow	299
Life is the hardest thing	195
Life pours down into the neon heart	237
Like the man who stands behind the man	33
Live fast be a spark and glow a while	341
Mary says she feels the Winter comin in	216
Momma doesn't like me	37
Money in my pocket down at Scream In Vain	285
My camera, sees things my eyes can't see	141
My friend she's on fire	194
My killer came in crinolines	127
Night fell fast, like it did in the past	202
O no another shit Saturday night	326
O yeah, o yeah, she come on like a hurricane	104
O you travelling ladies I do not believe you	156
Offices are emptying their pale-faced wards into the street	344
Oh, I don't wanna have to take you out	321
On a night like this I deserve to get kissed	301
On blind dates you meet in corners	65
Original Miss Jesus, yea she's always hanging 'round	254
Over there across the river	303

Pale white girls. Look for love	260
Put your head between your knees and breathe real deep	118
Say hi to Mick for me	284
Say what you want	223
Set the guitar control to stun	73
She keeps her lover on ice	340
She takes her face off and she puts it in a row	198
She's a lover and she fits inside my head	287
She's not the best, pretty-ish	289
Shine on, shine on me	291
Sighs and whispers, cries and whimpers	292
Silicon chip inside her head gets switched to overload	163
Sink with me beneath the waves	240
Sissy was a bright young thing	119
Sitting in the front row	215
Skin on Skin, nothing more nor less than	295
So I turned on the radio	200
Something's wrong, she was lying on the bed	161
Somewhere a screen door slammed	159
Somewhere up town late last night around 9 o'clock	225
Sooner or later when the dawn was breaking	184
Stop all your crying	143
Sweet thing you make my gums bleed	308
Take me back to Boomtown	273
Take my head and fuck with it	20
Tell me what you're doing coming in so late at night	238
Terry still meets Julie every Friday night	209
There was a lot of rocking going on that night	271
There's a full moon over Addis tonight	21
These are danger days	130
They won't break you with that heartless heart	313
This is the moment that we come alive	311
Though it strikes you as seeming a little absurd	114
Through tunnel vision watch him rant and rave	241
To live in love is all there is	318
To the bitter end we go all the way	64
Today in the park I thought I saw you	262
Too cruel to be true those dreams they had for you	68
Too late, it's too late God	323
Too late she cried	325
Traffic's wild tonight	93